The Pursuit of Liberty

Protecting our God-given Rights…
Before it is Too Late

The Pursuit of Liberty

Protecting our God-given Rights…
Before it is Too Late

Amy L. Travis

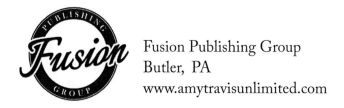

Fusion Publishing Group
Butler, PA
www.amytravisunlimited.com

ISBN 978-1-7335626-5-2

Printed in the United States of America

Published by Fusion Publishing Group
Butler, Pennsylvania

Visit https://www.amytravisunlimited.com/ or
email atravisconsulting@gmail.com

Edited by Mindi Stearns, Printworthy Proofreading
Photo credit on back cover: Marta Greca, MEDIA—The Creative Agency

TABLE OF CONTENTS

Dedication

To my husband, Perry Travis, the kindest,
most generous man I've ever known
and a true Patriot

Foreword
by Suzanne Austin

As a touring comedienne, I have literally traveled from one end of this continent to the other. I can tell you that the saying "we live in a crazy world" is an understatement. In the midst of this insanity, people all over the world are looking for peace, truth, and clarity.

There is a movement going on in our country. A revolution—if you will—of people who are waking up to truths hidden from us ALL for centuries. Thanks to those who seek the truth, more people are waking up, joining together, and fighting back against these evil entities.

When I read Amy's book, it was truly an awakening! She uses facts and extensive research to show how we have been "duped" by politicians, the corrupt media, Hollywood, and even well-meaning pastors and spiritual leaders. As she points out, the Bible talks about why capitalism works, why socialism always fails, and how to achieve true justice.

She goes on to say how "God is the author and defender of Justice. No one cares for the oppressed more than the Creator of the universe. America is headed down a very dark path if we continue to seek 'fundamental change' to the rule of law. The only way to enjoy true freedom in our country is to move back toward our Constitution, not away from it. The United States Constitution is the only governing system worldwide which ensures equal justice under the law—for all."

I first met Amy through our daughters' mutual friendship when I was searching for someone to help me publish my autobiography, *From Bags to Riches: One Woman's Journey from the Streets to the Stars*. My daughter told me her friend's mom was a published author. We met over dinner and, even though we came from completely different backgrounds, we clicked instantly. Amy is a follower of our Lord Jesus Christ and a true Patriot. She has been married to her awesome husband Perry for over 30 years, and they have three amazing adult children.

I immediately hired her to edit and publish mine. She took a mixed-up pile of crazy stories and created a literary masterpiece.

The Pursuit of Liberty not only made many things crystal clear and easy to understand, but it gave me hope. It reminded me that no matter what, God always has my back if I just do the next right thing. The good news about this Revolution is that Godly people are becoming staunch Patriots and warriors for truth, and Patriotic Americans are seeing these truths and finding their way to real relationships with God… thanks to people like Amy.

Reading her work was like riding a boat on a gentle wave in the midst of a raging storm.

Introduction

There is so much "noise" all around us. Loud voices are telling us what to think, who to believe, and how to feel. In recent years we've seen how the media attempts to control the narrative and suppress the facts. CEOs of the most prominent social media platforms confess to manipulating truth in order to control the thoughts and behaviors of their followers.

As believers in Jesus Christ, it is increasingly more difficult to know and understand the truth. Matthew 24:24 says, "For false messiahs and false prophets will rise up and perform great signs and wonders as to deceive, if possible, even God's chosen ones."

Our current situation reminds me of the climactic scene in the Wizard of Oz when Dorothy and her cohorts arrive at the Emerald City. The Great Wizard promised to grant their wishes if they could defeat the wicked witch. As they stand before the "Great and Powerful Oz" lights flash, fire explodes, and his voice booms. The anticipation builds as they know all of their hopes will finally be realized.

And then *it* happens. Dorothy's Yorkshire Terrier, Toto, wonders away and pulls back the curtain to reveal the shenanigans. There is no great and powerful Oz, just a man pushing buttons and flipping switches. They recognize in that moment that they've been duped.

And so have we. We've been duped by Hollywood, social media, and corporate America who tell us that money and power should be our gods, gender is fluid, America is racist, and capitalism is evil. Basically, facts do not matter and truth no longer exists.

The truth is that God created human beings in his image and likeness. He created them "male" and "female." Any attempts to redefine sexuality are dangerous and carry dire consequences. Gender is not a social construct; it's a biological reality. Pretending gender "is fluid" will sabotage healthy relationships and undermine the nuclear family.

In his infinite wisdom, God designed human beings to enjoy and benefit from relationships. No relationships are more important and vital to our health, wealth, and security than those within the family unit. Both adults and children experience great benefits from being part of a family; being separated leaves an individual exposed and vulnerable.

Regardless of the hate that surrounds us, our responsibility—particularly as Christians—to those in our culture who are lost and confused is to love and respect everyone, especially those who disagree with us. There are many ways to show kindness, grace, and compassion and one of the best ways is to forgive. We don't have to accept, however, that "love" means a blanket stamp of approval on every lifestyle. We can choose to love someone without liking their personal choices.

Right now, our nation is in crisis. America was built on the concept of personal freedom—the right to own property, peacefully assemble, worship God, build wealth, protect your family, and pursue happiness. But the very foundation of our society is eroding beneath our feet. Individuals who hate America are trying to suppress our freedoms, destroy our economy, and "fundamentally change" our nation to look more like Cuba or Venezuela—the very countries from which many citizens fled to come to America. If our Democracy falls, there will be nowhere left to go.

We have a systemic problem in our country, but it's not racism. It's poverty. Bad actors in government created systems of poverty in order to suppress entire generations of Americans. Those who created the crisis are claiming they have the solution to the very same problem. These are the same individuals dividing our nation across artificial lines and inflating the COVID-19 infection rates in order to keep us locked down.

The push to "defund the police" isn't about curing racial injustice, it's about creating chaos and seizing control. This movement mocks and silences anyone advocating for law and order. Make no mistake, the call to fundamentally change America is a naked grab for power and nothing more.

But the final verdict is not yet in. God is the author and defender of Justice. No one cares for the oppressed more than the Creator of the universe. True conservatism and the gospel of Jesus Christ are making a come-back in America. The only way to enjoy true freedom in our country is to move back *toward* our Constitution, not away from it. The United States Constitution is the only governing system worldwide which ensures equal justice under the law—for all.

There was a time in America when sincere believers in Jesus Christ could support the Democratic party with a clear conscience. Until around the 1980s, Democrats represented the working class. Both sides of my grandparents were registered Democrats their entire lives. Their families immigrated from Europe to find better opportunity. They were honest, hard-working, and devoutly religious.

However, in the last few decades the political left has abandoned its own people. The party who formerly advocated for the middle class now openly embraces late-term abortion, radical Marxist ideology, and is racing toward the legalization of infanticide (i.e., murder) and even pedophilia as part of the protected LGBTQ community. The California legislature, for example, passed a bill in September 2020 which would end automatic registry for some sex-offenders who commit sexual acts with minors.[1]

The window for plausible deniability for dedicated believers in Jesus who continue to support the Democrat party establishment has officially closed.

In contrast, the Trump Administration has done more in recent years to protect the unborn child, defend religious freedom, create economic opportunity for everyone, end sex-trafficking, preserve law and order, and fight for those truly oppressed by an unfair system created by greedy politicians. President Trump also relocated the US embassy to Jerusalem, a move the past two administrations promised but never delivered.

Christian conservativism is back.

This book is a call for us to look beyond all the smoke and mirrors; to ignore the hysteria which bombards us every day. Like Dorothy, we should "pay no attention to that man behind the curtain." When we have the privilege of looking at this from the other side we'll see how in the final analysis, regardless of lies and deception, God is right and his Word is truth.

In the end, we will recognize that God still reigns over the universe. It's His game, His rules. A time is coming when Truth will be revealed and all evil deeds will be exposed. Until then, we should continue our pursuit of true liberty.

1

The Frailty of Freedom

A merica. "The Land of the Free and the Home of the Brave."

You may recognize this as the last line in the Star-Spangled Banner written by Francis Scott Key as he watched a huge American flag raised by soldiers at Baltimore's Fort McHenry, after a critical victory over the British in 1814. This conflict, also referred to as the "Second War of Independence,"[2] was the first test of the new American republic.

The British had recently captured Washington D.C., burned the White House, and were now moving to invade Baltimore. They were confident that taking Baltimore—a thriving port city—would prove even more strategic than conquering the capital city. Major General Robert Ross, the commander of the British Army, felt certain that taking Baltimore would cripple the American war effort and provide a victory for England.[3]

With over ten thousand men and one hundred cannons, the Americans mounted a stronger defense than anticipated. British warships were pressed to engage and they bombarded Fort McHenry with mortar fire. However, because of the shallow waters surrounding the Port of Baltimore, the British fleet eventually withdrew. The defeat of the British at Fort McHenry in Baltimore was a decisive victory for the Americans and led to both sides signing a peace agreement later that same year.[4]

⋆ ᵴᵵᵵᵴᵴ • ᵶᵶᵶᵶᵶ ⋆

Unfortunately, many may not recognize that these famous lyrics from the Star-Spangled Banner were penned as a result of that fateful battle. In recent years there's been a coordinated effort to erase history and reshape the narrative in our country. We are seeing individuals disrespecting our flag, desecrating our monuments, and erasing the brave heroes who fought for our freedom.

During the summer of 2020, over 104 statues and monuments commemorating our American history were vandalized. Statues of Confederate and Union soldiers alike have been toppled, defaced, or decapitated in Minnesota, Alabama, Florida, Georgia, Illinois, New York, Oregon, Texas, Louisiana, Virginia, California, and Washington, D.C. Although these acts were committed under the guise of protesting our country's racist roots, many statues attacked by vandals had nothing to do with slavery or racism, such as the 120-year-old statue of an elk in Portland, Oregon.[5]

Petitions are being filed with the U.S. House of Representatives to remove "under God" from the Pledge of Allegiance for all schools. Advocates of this view believe schools are forcing students to "believe in God" by allowing the phrase to remain in the pledge.[6] These individuals contend this verbiage violates their First Amendment rights.

The "Land of the Free" is facing unprecedented challenges that threaten our freedoms. Our heritage is being uprooted daily.

America's uniqueness lies in the fact that it is the only country expressly founded on the idea of religious freedom. The early settlers to America risked their lives and their children's lives to make the treacherous journey across the Atlantic Ocean in search of this elusive target. It's highly unlikely that any of us in this country will experience the persecution and torture for our religious beliefs that those first Americans did back in England.

This persecution—including the seizing of land and assets and physical torture—came at the hands of the state-run church.

Now think about that for a minute. State-run church. We're not talking about the Methodist church of Pennsylvania. State-run churches, also known as state-sponsor religions, grant power to the government to tax, punish, torture, or kill you for not conforming to their laws. And let's be clear about this—state-run religions have absolutely nothing to do with God. State-run religion is a means of controlling the population.

In 1776, the United States of America declared independence from the oppressive, totalitarian British government, sparking the Revolutionary War. The men who signed this document understood the risk they were taking to secure their own freedom and the freedom of many generations to come. This heroic act didn't go without notice. England branded these men as traitors and hunted them down like animals. According to historian Allan Hicks,

Five signers were captured by the British as traitors, and tortured before they died. Twelve had their homes ransacked and burned. Two lost their sons serving in the Revolutionary Army; another had two sons captured. Nine of the 56 fought and died from wounds or hardships of the Revolutionary War.[7]

In countries all around the world, government replaces God. There are no freedoms—religious, personal, or otherwise—because an individual has no rights. The government controls all the wealth, all the resources, all the land, all the people, all the time.

Consider nations where state-sponsored or state-run religions still exist: Afghanistan, Algeria, Egypt, Iran, Iraq, Jordan, Kuwait, Libya, Malaysia, Pakistan, Saudi Arabia, and Yemen, for example, have Islam as their state-sponsored religion. Also, in Cambodia, Sri Lanka, and Thailand, Buddhism is the state-sponsored religion. These countries are notorious for consistently and systematically violating human rights.

Unlike the horrific violations of basic human rights perpetuated by governments all over the world, the United States' Constitution grants us PERSONAL freedom. We have the ability to live where we want, pursue any career we want, and make as much money as we can. We can go to church anywhere we would like and practice any religion we choose.

This is why the Declaration of America's Independence from England was, and still is, so radical. No other nation on the face of the earth had ever granted such freedom to their citizens. The document signed by Congress on July 4, 1776 contains the following statement:

> *We hold these truths to be self-evident, that all men are created equal, that they are endowed by their Creator with certain unalienable Rights, that among these are Life, Liberty and the pursuit of Happiness.*

As difficult as it may be to comprehend, personal freedom—the right to own property, to build wealth, to protect yourself and your family, and to pursue happiness—didn't exist prior to 1776. The Founding Fathers who secured our independence from England were conducting a social experiment called America.

In 1787, four years after the newly formed American army defeated the British in the Revolutionary War, the Founding Fathers drafted the Constitution to establish rules for the novel government. These laws were based on the idea that God created the universe and thus is the only one who can give life and take it away—not the government. The creators of the Constitution patterned the new form of governing after the ideals found in Scripture: freedom to worship, sacredness of human life, the ability to own private property, the traditional family, and free markets.

The need for freedom of religion was front-and-center when the Constitution was written. The founders understood the undeniable connection between religious freedom, capitalism, property rights, and prosperity.

Contrary to popular opinion, the notion of the separation of church and state isn't a liberal ideology, it references the First Amendment to the Constitution:

Amendment I

Congress shall make no law respecting an establishment of religion or prohibiting the free exercise thereof; or abridging the freedom of speech, or of the press; or the right of the people peaceably to assemble, and to petition the government for a redress of grievances.

Previously, the church and state were the same thing. Government was intended to be sovereign—our provider, our security, and our savior. Separating the two entities in this new government system allowed the individual freedom to worship the Creator, not the government.

The amazing thing about our Constitution is that it guarantees freedom for all religions. Americans are free to practice their faith as Jews, Christians, Muslims, Buddhists, and the like, as long as it is done peacefully and within the boundaries of the law.

Governed by God

Fast-forward two hundred years. In post-postmodern America there is a notion that separation of church and state means that government and governing institutions should not be influenced by Christianity *in any way*. Advocates for this erroneous interpretation of the church-and-state debate have been slowly pecking away at the foundation of our Constitution, especially with respect to freedom of religion.

There is no factual or historical basis for the removal of Christianity from the Rule of Law in America. As mentioned above, our Constitution is built on the foundation of biblical Christianity. The brave young men who rebelled against the tyrannical government in England understood this truth.

William Penn, the colonist who purchased Pennsylvania said, "Men must be governed by God or they will be ruled by tyrants." Penn's hope for Pennsylvania was for it to become a refuge for Quakers and other persecuted people groups. He had a vision for building an ideal Christian commonwealth.[8]

Like many others, Penn understood that if we reject the protections offered through the natural order which God established at creation, we leave ourselves open to be exploited by power-hungry dictators and oppressors.

Make no mistake. It is *impossible* to separate Christianity from politics. Did you know that 37 of the 39 books of the Old Testament in the Bible were written to, about, or by political leaders? The historical books of the Old Testament outline the founding, establishment, and subsequent fall of the nation of Israel. We see kings, judges, tribal elders, and oppressive foreign governments mentioned throughout Scripture.

Moses established local governments to rule over the millions of Israelites in their temporary camps.

[Moses] chose capable men from all over Israel and appointed them as leaders over the people. He put them in charge of groups of one thousand, one hundred, fifty, and ten. These men were always available to solve the people's common

disputes. They brought the major cases to Moses, but they took care of the smaller matters themselves (Exodus 18:26-28).

Prophets in ancient days served as consultants to kings. They were political advisors! They were not men with long robes that stood at the entrance to the temple and chanted. And as we see with Jeremiah, Nathan, and Ezra, many of them had a seat at the table and the ability to direct both foreign and domestic policy. The prophet Nehemiah served on the cabinet for the Persian King Artaxerxes and eventually led a coalition of Jews to return to Israel after years of living in exile.

It's Not Me, It's You

Please don't be fooled. The fight to extrapolate Christianity from modern society isn't an innocent misunderstanding or the expression of another viewpoint, it's a coup attempt. America is under siege. The attempt to obscure Christianity in American government by some in leadership is part of a larger plan to "fundamentally transform America" by creating separation between modern America and the Constitution.

When disenfranchised young people, graduates of our state-run colleges and universities, began vandalizing and tearing down historic monuments and statues, they weren't protesting American's racist roots. If this were true, they wouldn't have toppled the statue of a Catholic priest and Abraham Lincoln, the man accredited with liberating the slaves.[9]

No, the rioters were protesting our *Christian* roots, not our racists roots.

Furthermore, it is important to understand that every government is guided by some type of belief system. Democracy is shaped by Christian principles. In contrast, Communism is guided by Marxism, and Sharia Law is directed by Islam.

Sharia Law, as observed in Saudi Arabia, Afghanistan, Iraq, and many other countries in Asia and Africa, extracts guidance from the Quran on penalties for behavior. For example, theft is punishable by amputation of the hands (Quran 5:38).[10]

Separation Anxiety

Many Americans are confused about the need for creating barriers between religious institutions and the government. These are the same individuals removing the Ten Commandments from walls of courtrooms. They reason that separating church and state means our legal system shouldn't be influenced by Christianity. But the separation of church and state was never about protecting the government from the church! Many in power today would like us to believe that, but it's simply not true.

The purpose of separating the church and state was *to protect individuals from the government, not the other way around.* Separation of church and state was always intended to guard our personal freedoms, not to protect the government from Christianity.

Perhaps the most disturbing finding is that historically, when a government deliberately rejects Judeo-Christian principles—such as capitalism and free markets, the sanctity of human life, and the ability of private citizens to own property—it does not bode well for that country's citizens.

We'll discuss these principles more in upcoming chapters.

Just within the last one hundred years we've seen the rejection of these principles of governance in Germany, Cuba, Venezuela, and North Korea.

In 1960, one of the first things the rebel leaders did during the revolution in Cuba was to cut off the food supply, as a means of forcing submission. Shortly after that, they destroyed churches and killed pastors because religion is viewed as an enemy of the state. The regime was confident that if they could indoctrinate the people—particularly the youth—Communism would take a firm hold in the hearts and minds of the Cuban people.

I was surprised to discover that even Germany was a democracy prior to 1933. Hitler and other Nazi leaders disrupted the democratic process by burning down the Reichstag, their parliamentary building, one week before the election was to take place.[11] Hitler capitalized on the chaos to seize power. Within the next forty-eight hours, he unlawfully imprisoned and tortured four thousand of his political enemies.[12]

German society, which previously valued human life, was soon replaced with Hitler's version of Darwinism. Evolutionary theory suggests that different races of people evolved at different times and rates, causing one race to be superior to another. And while some don't believe Darwin ever fully envisioned the consequences of this flawed line of thinking, many believe Adolf Hitler's obsession with racial purity and the demonization of the Jews was fueled by Darwin's conjecture.

We all know what happened soon after that with the ethnic cleansing campaign that began with the elimination of its most vulnerable populations: the sick, elderly, and children.

When Christianity and its governing principles are removed from government, individual rights and freedoms are *always* sacrificed in the process.

The Fall of Democracy

It's hard to imagine that our beautiful Democracy in America—built and paid for by the blood and sweat of the brave founders—could ever be destroyed. But history tells us otherwise.

Even the mighty Roman empire fell, the superpower that encompassed much of the known world for over five hundred years. Historians don't agree on the precise reasons, but most concur that political corruption and over-spending were significant reasons.

How exactly does a democracy fall? We have seen from history that three major factors contribute to the fall of a democratic society:

1. Deny religious freedom through fear and intimidation.

2. Ruin the economy through extreme taxation, oppressive regulations, and replacing private enterprise with inefficient government oversight.

3. Allow bad-actors into government, thus increasing wide-spread corruption.

Simply put, any attempt to topple a democratic governing system is a play for power.

We should be very concerned when some in our government are attempting to remove our history, destroy capitalism, and "fundamentally change" our society. These attempts have nothing to do with social justice and have everything to do with ushering in a dictatorial power within government.

Major Amir Tsarfati, a decorated officer in the Israeli Army, said in a *Happening Now* event in Southern California, "Socialism always comes to power in a semi-democratic way but will never let go of power until there is bloodshed. I've seen it many times all over the world."[13]

The Wrap-Up

America was founded on the idea of religious freedom. But Democracy—government by the people and for the people—is under attack in America. Our freedom to worship our Creator in any way we choose is the primary cornerstone on which this country was built, but it is slowly eroding away.

Unfortunately, not all Americans recognize what is at stake here. The loss of freedom of religion is more tragic than we could imagine.

Worldwide, biblically based Christianity is the only religious system that supports personal freedom and is compatible with a democratic government. Attempts to remove Christian values by a government are a coordinated effort to suppress individual rights and usher in a dictatorship.

The separation of church and state is intended to protect citizens—to protect you and me—from unlawful interference by the government in private matters, including the freedom to worship. The government replaces God in systems such as socialism, Communism, Marxism, and others. When Christian principles are removed and a democratic system of government is replaced with socialism, it never goes well for that country's citizens.

I recently spoke with a friend whose family escaped from Cuba in the early 2000s. His words were very chilling. He said, "If America's great Democracy falls, there will be no place left to go."

If we allow our Constitution to be compromised and our Christian roots upended, we will suffer the fate of other failed countries—the very nations from which our citizens originally fled in pursuit of liberty.

Discussion Guide

Chapter 1: The Frailty of Freedom

The purpose of this section is to help you facilitate meaningful discussion surrounding the material in this chapter.

1. Can you summarize the main idea of this chapter?

2. Consider this statement from the Declaration of Independence: "We hold these truths to be self-evident, that all men are created equal, that they are endowed by their Creator with certain unalienable Rights, that among these are Life, Liberty and the pursuit of Happiness." Do other countries uphold this standard? Have you been to countries who do not?

3. Discuss the idea of "separation of church and state." How do you interpret this statement? Do you agree or disagree with the author's interpretation?

4. Many Christians point to Romans 13 as a basis for respecting government authority. Do you think that applies all the time? What do you think would have happened if the men who fought for America's independence would have taken that position toward the British Government?

5. Do you agree or disagree with the statement: "It is impossible to separate Christianity from government?" Give examples of your position.

6. What do you think people mean when they say they want to fundamentally change America?

Scriptures to read and discuss:

- Romans 13:1–5
- 1 Timothy 2:1–2
- Galatians 5:1
- 1 Peter 2:16
- 1 Thessalonians 5:12
- Romans 13:7

Video: A video on this subject entitled "Should Church and State be Separate" is available on the FUSION Leadership Group Site:
https://www.fusionleadership.site/toughquestionseries

2

Family Matters

One of my heroes is my mother-in-law, Mary-Ann Travis. My husband Perry is the fourth of five sons in the Travis family. Mary-Ann had the unenviable task of raising five boys on her own after her husband left when the youngest son was a year old.

With little help from government assistance programs, Mary-Ann worked several jobs in order to feed her family and keep their home. The older sons needed to pitch in to the family finances, too. Perry recalls his older brothers handing over their paychecks from their high school jobs to mom to pay the bills. Christmas and birthdays were pretty lean, as you may imagine.

In spite of the immense challenges she faced, Mary-Ann was one of the kindest and most compassionate individuals I have ever met. She was quick to forgive, even those who hurt her deeply. If you knew her, you understood that—next to her sons—her faith in Jesus Christ was the most important thing in her life. And if you didn't know this, she would be sure to tell you. Mary-Ann would walk up to strangers in restaurants to talk about Jesus, and she would pray for the local plumber before she would let him conclude his service call.

Perry would call or visit his mom every Father's Day, in addition to the typical holidays. She had to be both mom and dad, a task that she took seriously. Mary-Ann took literally the promise in Psalm 68:5–6 that God was her husband.

Father to the fatherless, defender of widows—
this is God, whose dwelling is holy.
God places the lonely in families;
he sets the prisoners free and gives them joy.

Momma Travis went to be with Jesus on January 2, 2019. I will forever remember her kindness to me and her faithfulness to God.

Love and Marriage

The family is the earliest institution established. God created man in his image. He created the woman so man wouldn't have to be alone, and He gave them both the command to be fruitful and multiply. The Creator of the universe could have populated the earth any way He wanted, but He chose to create families.

God created the family for the purpose of protecting and preserving its participants. We understand how children benefit from the family unit, but the same is true for adults, too.

Both secular and faith-based studies on health and wellness conclude the same thing: marriage is beneficial to the individual. Consider a study from Harvard Medical

School first published in 2010 and updated in 2019 that discusses married men and mortality. The survey of over 120,000 individuals found that married men are healthier than unmarried, widowed, or divorced men.[14]

The study also concluded that marriage has a positive effect on a variety of health outcomes, specifically mental health. Married men have a lower risk of depression, reduced risk of Alzheimer's disease, improved blood sugar levels, and a greater probability of recovering from serious physical conditions.[15]

Remarkably, the same or similar results were discovered in countries all over the world. In addition to the American study, Great Britain and Japan also recorded findings that marriage was positively linked to greater health outcomes.

Some of these studies went so far as to suggest that the quality of the marriage had little effect. Married men with poor relationships with their spouse still enjoyed greater health and happiness than their never married or divorced counterparts.

Other studies have concluded that marriage is a surprising predictor of wealth.[16] A study from the University of Michigan concluded that "getting married increases wealth and income."[17] Even those who disparage marriage, for one reason or another, have a difficult time explaining away this phenomenon.

If adults fare better within the family unit, it goes without saying that the benefit for children is even greater. Children in two-parent households are more likely to get As in school, enjoy school, and enroll in extracurricular activities. As teenagers, these children are less likely to abuse drugs, drop out of school, and have children outside of marriage.

Orphans, on the other hand, have always been and always will be the most vulnerable population of any society.

In recent years, my family has enjoyed the pleasure of being involved with an orphanage in Kagadi, Uganda in East Africa. On our first trip to Uganda in 2018 we met Robert and Milly Kikomeko, a young couple who started a school/orphanage at their own expense to care for the growing number of vulnerable children in Robert's native village. Uganda has one of the highest orphan populations in the entire world—largely due to the AIDS epidemic in this region—with more than 12% of all children likely to end up on the streets or worse.[18]

Robert and Milly recognized that children who are compromised because of the absence of parents or a dysfunctional family situation are at much greater risk to be abandoned, abused, or trafficked—including the practice of childhood marriages, still common in rural Uganda. As a result of the compassion and dedication of this one couple, over four hundred and fifty children are cared for at Maisha School and Orphanage. We love Robert and Milly so much that we've unofficially adopted them into our own family.

Closer to Home

Here at home we face a different epidemic that threatens our society—the absence of fathers. The lack of a father in the home poses very serious risks to the health and wellbeing of a child.

Poverty is regarded as the greatest risk for families without a father at home. Women-only households are significantly more likely than two-parent households to live below the poverty line. Children from these families are vulnerable to many hardships, both economic and social, throughout their lives.[19]

Statistics from the U.S. Department of Health and Human Services, Bureau of the Census, and other government sites tell the following story:

- 63% of youth suicides are from fatherless homes
- 85% of children who show behavior disorders come from fatherless homes
- 90% of all homeless and runaway children come from fatherless homes
- 80% of those convicted of rape and other violent offenses come from fatherless homes
- 85% of all youth in prison are from fatherless homes

Special thanks to Sabrina, author of The Fatherless Generation Project for collecting these statistics from government websites.[20]

I would like to acknowledge that many, many adult children who grew up without fathers have overcome the challenges and live fruitful, productive lives. Many of these men, like my husband, develop a greater commitment to their children and families as a result of being abandoned by their own fathers. Some will tell you, however, that having male role models and mentors made all the difference in their lives. The brutal truth is that fathers, even more than mothers, have a direct and undeniable impact on their offspring.

Fatherhood Failures

Tragically, absent fathers and the problems associated with them have adversely affected the black community more than any other ethnic group in our country.

Jack Brewer, a former NFL player with the New York Giants, is also an evangelist who has initiated a prison ministry through his foundation. Brewer acknowledges that as many as 77% of babies born in the black community are born to single moms. "The number of kids who don't have fathers or positive male influences is devasting," according to Brewer. "Our institutionalized system has made this acceptable in black culture today."[21]

Brewer's Foundation has implemented programs to teach business and leadership skills to incarcerated men. Brewer is committed to bridging the gap of missing fathers within the black community through improved legislation and rehabilitation. This course offered through the prison systems in Texas qualifies under the First Step Act[22] enacted under the Trump Administration to give reduced sentences to men who successfully complete the program.

"The program is about rehabilitation, but at the core, it's about fatherhood. We talk about not just the father in the flesh, but about our Father in heaven."[23]

Under Attack

Given the extraordinary, God-given protection offered to both adults and children, it's no wonder that the family structure and institution are under attack. God created the family to protect and preserve its participants. It only makes sense that Satan would seek to destroy the family.

In an early experiment with socialism in America in 1826, Robert Owen—originally from England—purchased property in Harmony, Indiana, and set up a colony which he said would produce morally superior human beings. Owen called the settlement "New Harmony."

Owen proclaimed the liberation of humankind would happen through the elimination of the "Trinity of Evils" responsible for all of humanity's misery: traditional religion, *conventional marriage*, and private property. Owen's prescription for paradise included abolishing the church, disrupting the family structure, and eliminating capitalism. His social experiment in America was a spectacular failure and he moved back to England.[24] We'll explore socialism in detail in Chapter 7.

Historically, any attempt to usurp the natural order of marriage and family leaves its members vulnerable and results in chaos.

China, for example, instituted its one-child policy in 1979 designed to systematically decrease the growing population of China. This policy imposed harsh consequences for families with multiple children, thereby encouraging parents to give up—and even kill—their daughters in order to have a son to carry on their family name. Families who defied the policy were punished with financial sanctions or worse. Many women were forced to have IUD insertions, abortions, and even sterilizations.[25]

This policy has had devastating consequences on the family structure in China. Families are experiencing the four-two-one problem. There are four grandparents and two parents who will look to a single child for care and financial support. Also, the intended and unintended consequences of this policy left China with significantly more males than females. Hundreds of single men of marriageable age are competing for one woman. Family life as we know it will be extinct in China within a matter of generations.

China is not the only country to experiment with the family structure. In the last ten years Cuba has become a haven for the LGBT community. This may seem like a victory for human rights, but it's not. Raul Castro supports homosexuality as a means of population control. Less babies being born will eventually lower the population on the island. In addition, encouraging the breakdown of the traditional family will isolate more individuals, thus strengthening the regime's hold on its citizens.

America is in the midst of its own social experiment seeking to disrupt and uproot the traditional family. The political organization Black Lives Matters (BLM) is masquerading as an advocate for minorities and under-served communities, but that's not their mission.

BLM's intended mission is to "disrupt the Western-prescribed nuclear family structure requirement."[26] This objective is very different from what most Americans believe about the Black Lives Matters movement. Many in minority communities have jumped on the bandwagon believing that BLM is supporting them. But, rather than advocating for black families and communities, the group has a very different agenda.

It's shocking, actually, to see what this group is up to. According to their mission statement, BLM is intended to "make space for transgenders to lead, and to disman-tle the patriarchal practice of mothers caring for their children so that they have time to protest for social justice." Their website states their true intention—namely, freeing themselves from the tight grip of "heteronormative think-ing." We'll explore this more in Chapter 4.

The irony of their name can be seen in the destruc-tion this group has caused in minority communities. BLM has undermined law and order by burning black-owned businesses and demanding the defunding of the police. It stands to reason that those who suffer most when police protection is taken away are vulnerable women and children.

The Wrap-Up

A wise man once said, "Family is the original Department of Health, Welfare, and Education."[27] God designed the family to protect and strengthen its partic-ipants—to protect us! Health, wealth, and companion-ship are some of the greatest advantages the family offers. Everyone within the family unit benefits both physically and emotionally when the family remains intact.

Thankfully, many brave individuals have learned to thrive, despite all of the challenges associated with divorce, abandonment, and the general breakdown of their families.

Fathers play a monumental role in the family struc-ture. The absence of fathers can be directly tied to poverty, crime, and hopelessness for the women and children they leave behind. Men face enormous pressures and challeng-es in today's society which threaten their own livelihoods, as well.

Satan, the "father of lies,"[28] seeks to destroy the institution of the family. His plan is to leave men, women, and children exposed and vulnerable. He infiltrates societies, governments, and individuals to spread his lies and deception.

There is a beautiful, but haunting, promise in the book of Malachi. Verse 4:6 says, "[God's] preaching will turn the hearts of fathers to their children, and the hearts of children to their fathers. Otherwise I will come and strike the land with a curse."

This we know for certain—family matters!

Discussion Guide

Chapter 2: Family Matters

The purpose of this section is to help you facilitate a meaningful discussion surrounding the material in this chapter.

1. Can you summarize the main idea of this chapter?

2. What was most surprising to you about the statistics regarding marriage and health?

3. Why do you think married men live longer, according to the statistics?

4. Consider the statement, "Family is the original Department of Health, Welfare, and Education." Can you give an example of how the family unit protects, provides care, or educates an adult or child?

5. Do you agree or disagree with the premise that the absence of fathers is a major problem in America? Provide examples to make your case.

6. How can we as individuals or collectively as the church help the "fatherless"?

Scriptures to explore:

- Deuteronomy 6:6–7
- Acts 16:31
- 1 Corinthians 1:10
- Proverbs 6:20
- 1 John 4:20
- Proverbs 3:11–12

3

The Rights of Life

In December of 2005, I ran into a friend I hadn't seen in years at a local coffee shop. At the time, I had no idea the lasting impact that chance meeting would have. Susan (we'll call her), normally vibrant and happy, was really distraught that day. After a little small talk, she relayed the bad news she received that week. She and her husband had tried for years to have a baby, without success. Once the medical options were exhausted, a plan was finally in place to adopt a child through a local agency. They were scheduled to pick up the child the following week when they received the call—the birth mom changed her mind. After months and months of prayer and paperwork, when the end was in sight, their hope changed in an instant. Susan was crushed.

Within a week of speaking with Susan, I ran into another friend. I saw this woman consistently and we often had brief conversations, usually about the weather and other unimportant stuff. On this day, Sandi (we'll call her) confided that she was in a tough spot: she was pregnant to a man she wasn't married to. She already had two children and couldn't imagine how she could care for a third. When she broke the news to her boyfriend, he ended the relationship and refused to see her.

Sandi held the conviction that abortion was not an option, so she was looking for someone to adopt her baby. A family member had originally agreed to adopt the child, but he and his wife had just backed out of the arrangement only days before we spoke.

As I listened, I tried hard not to jump out of my chair. After a while I told her that I knew someone who may want to adopt her baby and asked her permission to speak to my friend. If she was interested, I promised to connect them. Sandi was excited about the prospect and gave me permission to bring up the subject with my friend.

I will never forget making that call on Christmas Eve. It must have been hard to conceal my excitement because Susan later said she knew why I was calling, even before I told her. The two women met together shortly thereafter, and the rest is history. The baby girl born in March of 2007 was adopted by Susan and her husband. God had—once again—worked out a solution to the problem for ALL the women, even before they were aware of their dilemmas.

There are a lot of social issues in America today which the Bible doesn't have any direct answers, but the case for protecting innocent life isn't one of them. Genesis 1 proclaims that God made man in his image; Exodus 20 records the Sixth Commandment, "You must not murder"; and Psalm 139 declares boldly and beautifully how life begins at conception. Very severe warnings are given against those who would harm children in both the Old Testament and the New Testament. Luke 17:2, for example, states: "It would be better for them to be thrown into the sea with a millstone tied around their neck than to cause one of these little ones to stumble" (NIV).

There is no room for "gray area" in the Christian worldview regarding abortion.

One of the more perplexing divisions of our times is between those who promote abortion (women's choice) and those who advocate for life. In 1973, the now-famous United States Supreme Court case *Roe v. Wade* ruled that access to safe and legal abortion is a constitutional right. This legislation became an extension of the idea that government shouldn't be able to tell women what to do with their bodies. Ever since that time, a battle has ensued.

Because all life is deemed sacred by God, many have taken up the cause of protecting the unborn. The pro-life movement started and was fueled by the Catholic Church which was among the first to recognize that life is a God-given privilege. In 1968, Pope Paul VI forbid abortion and most methods of birth control.[29]

Although this stance has been disputed in recent days, many within the Catholic Church still valiantly defend the rights of the unborn child. Sister Deirdre Bryne proudly represents the best of this community. In a speech she gave in August 2020 to a national audience, Sister Dede, a retired Army officer and surgeon, discussed her work serving the poor in Haiti, Sudan, Kenya, and Iraq. She talked about how the refugees she has worked with have been marginalized, viewed as insignificant, and have been deemed powerless.

The largest marginalized group in the world, though, Sister Dede stated, are not outside our borders. They are here in the United States and they are the unborn.[30]

Toward the end of the 1970s, evangelical Christians joined the movement.[31] As late as the 1960s, pastors and evangelical scholars couldn't agree if abortion was sinful. But thanks to the groundbreaking work done by our Catholic brothers and sisters, the sentiment changed. More and more evangelical organizations such as Students for Life of America, Concerned Women for America, the Family Research Council, and others joined the fight. For the next few decades, the focus shifted from saving babies at all costs, to educating and supporting women in crisis. During this time, the "face" of the movement changed to become characterized by white, suburban conservatives.

The *Roe v. Wade* legislation remained uncontested for several decades. But on October 2, 2003, under President George Bush, the Partial-Birth Abortion Ban Act was passed to ban certain procedures deemed to be cruel and barbaric. This decision marked the first time since 1973 that any restrictions were placed on abortion.[32]

In recent years, however, there has been a push to overturn the ban on late-term abortions. Laws preventing healthcare providers from performing abortions in the third trimester of a woman's pregnancy has been the only restraint on the very lucrative industry. Abortion providers pull in US $1.3 billion annually.[33]

Rather than continued progress toward making abortion illegal, many proponents are choosing to double down. The push toward political correctness has caused the unthinkable murder of viable, unborn babies to become more acceptable. Some in the media seek to change what they deem to be the offensive labeling of "pro-choice" and "pro-life" to include more neutral phrases such "abortion-rights advocates" and "abortion-rights opponents."[34] Advocates for abortion on demand are offended by the term "pro-life," possibly because it implies that unborn children have rights, not just the activists.

Here is what I do not understand: Why isn't adoption being pushed as an alternative to late-term abortion? As a human being, partial-birth abortion doesn't make sense to me on any level. But as a mother, it makes even less sense. Why would any woman purposely go through nine months of pregnancy if they had even an inkling that they want to abort? Pregnancy is no fun. I can't imagine any rational, caring woman willingly choosing to kill the child they carried for the past nine months, rather than seeking a plan for adoption.

You may not realize this if you've never had the need, but every state in the United Sates has Safe Haven laws. This means that a mother, and even a father, can relinquish an unharmed baby to any hospital without risk of being prosecuted for child abandonment. Many states have gone to great lengths to ensure privacy to protect both the child and the person relinquishing them.[35]

With so many other legitimate, legal, and humane options, why is late-term, partial-birth abortion still even up for discussion? This indicates to me that something else is at play in this situation.

The country's largest provider of abortions is the infamous organization, Planned Parenthood. If you go to the Planned Parenthood (PP) website, you'll read how the organization was founded in 1916 on the idea that women should have "the information and care they need to live strong, healthy lives, and fulfill their dreams."[36] This notion is easily debunked, however, when you begin to investigate further.

I remember being shown a video in fifth grade from Planned Parenthood demonstrating how women "have a choice." I will never forget coming home and telling my mom, very nonchalantly, about the woman in the video. When told by the doctor that she was having a girl, she immediately declared that she wanted an abortion because she already had two girls. The doctor agreed that this was a good option and scheduled her appointment.

My mom was OUTRAGED. I had never seen her freak out like that—before or since. My teacher Mr. Aufmann received a call from at least one angry parent that day. I didn't understand her reaction at the time, but I do now.

Planned Parenthood's motivation for "helping" women becomes clear—and disturbing—when you learn about the company's founder, Margaret Sanger. Sanger was a believer in eugenics, the idea of creating a superior society by encouraging procreation among the higher classes, and discouraging it among the poor and uneducated classes.[37] As a resident of New York City, Sanger first implemented her "Negro Project" by establishing a birth control clinic in Harlem, a predominantly black neighborhood, in 1923.[38] In short, Sanger sought to reduce or eliminate the black population through various birth control methods, including abortion.[39]

Even today, 62% of Planned Parenthood's abortion clinics are located in "targeted neighborhoods" where there is a high African American population.[40]

Sanger's influence on the African American community is tragic. Each year more African American children are aborted in New York City than are born.[41] Even abortion activist groups such as the Guttmacher Institute admit that black women are more than five times as likely as white women to have an abortion.[42]

New Life for the Pro-Life Movement

A new trend has recently started. After years of being championed by the Catholic Church and Evangelical believers, predominantly from suburban churches, there is new life for the pro-life movement. Joining the fight are influential, Conservative-Christian men from the black community who recognize that their population has suffered the most from Planned Parenthood's targeting of poor black neighborhoods.

In 2019, Kayne West declared his pro-life views in a radio interview promoting his new album *Jesus Is King*. West, the highest-paid rapper in 2019, admits that the black community has been "brainwashed" by progressive policies that advocated for them aborting their children.[43] His own father, he confessed, wanted him aborted.[44] This new stance represents a major swing for West who openly promoted abortion in his 2013 song "Blood on the Leaves" as a way to avoid consequences of extramarital affairs and the responsibility of fatherhood.[45] The new-and-improved Kanye 2.0 has breathed new life into an old debate.

Also joining the fight is David J. Harris, Jr., author of *Why I Couldn't Stay Silent: One Man's Battle as a Black Conservative.*[46] In the book, Harris shares his deeply rooted conviction about the right for life as a conservative, as a believer, and as a father. In fact, he feels so strongly about the pro-life, anti-abortion position that he asserts that it is the single most important issue when it comes to voting.[47]

Many from every ethnic and socioeconomic class are finally coming to understand that abortion is not healthcare; it's genocide—a coordinated and systematic killing of a racial or cultural group.

Others pushing back against the abortion industry include Pastors Jay and Tiffany Gilbert of Another Level Ministries in Pittsburgh, Pennsylvania. The Gilberts opened East Liberty Women's Care Center in the spring of 2021 to give young women facing unplanned pregnancies an alternative to abortion. The center provides support for *all* family members and is strategically placed just one block from the largest abortion provider in the region.

The Gilberts are teaming up with other churches, local authorities, and several conservative judges to speak up for those who cannot speak for themselves. According to Pastor Jay, "It's time to stop playing church and start being the church."

The Role of Rules

What about the argument that it is unconstitutional for the government to tell women what they can and cannot do with their bodies? This is considered the basis for the legal argument of *Roe v. Wade.*

Consider this: In a state where there are no restrictions on abortion—such as New York—a mother could legally abort her son or daughter the day before her due date. If, however, en route to the abortion clinic a driver strikes her car, killing her and her unborn child, the driver could be charged with *two* counts of vehicular manslaughter. The absurdity and irony of this hypocrisy in our legal system is breathtaking.

If a pregnant woman is legally considered to be two separate people, it stands to reason that her "rights to her own body" end where the next life begins.

For this reason, many states have begun adopting the Human Rights Protection Act, more commonly known as the *Heartbeat Bill*. This legislation bans abortion as soon as a fetal heartbeat can be detected, as early as six weeks into pregnancy. This bill allows for exceptions when the life of the mother is in jeopardy, but not for rape and incest cases. Under this law, doctors who violate these terms could incur criminal penalties.[48] As of this writing, Georgia, Kentucky, Louisiana, Mississippi, and Missouri have passed this bill or one similar.

The government of any developed nation has both a right and responsibility to protect all citizens, especially those who cannot speak for themselves. The primary role of government is to restrain evil, according to John Eidsmoe, author of *God and Caesar: Biblical Faith and Political Action* (Wipf and Stock Publishers, 1997). The fight for life is not only constitutional, it is also the obligation of any citizen of the kingdom of heaven.

America is in a fight for her lives.

Discussion Guide

Chapter 3: The Rights of Life

The purpose of this section is to help you facilitate a meaningful discussion surrounding the material in this chapter.

1. Can you summarize the main idea of this chapter?

2. What does the term "eugenics" mean?

3. Do you think the government has the right to place restrictions on abortion? Why or why not?

4. Many have said that abortion is the primary issue they use to determine which candidate to vote for. Do you agree or disagree? Make your case for why or why not.

5. According to John Eidsmoe, "The primary role of government is to restrain evil." Name some other areas or policy issues where this idea already is or should be applied.

6. How can we, collectively or individually, encourage adoption in our culture over abortion?

Scriptures to read and discuss:

- Psalm 139 (entire chapter)
- Proverbs 19:8
- Galatians 2:20
- Genesis 9:5–6
- Ephesians 5:15–16
- Proverbs 25:26

4

Gender Reveal

An incident that happened when my son Nick was in eighth grade. He was called to the principal's office after another student reported him for a comment he made. Nick was surprised by the summons, and not exactly sure what he did wrong. The assistant principal explained that another student was offended because he told her that *there were only two genders.* The school administrator then went on to inform him that the government just published a listing of over fifty-one genders (this was in 2016 during the Obama Administration), and that he has no right to challenge this.

Nick—just being Nick—said, "No, there's only two genders. You can't convince me otherwise." Eventually the administrator let him off with a warning and told him that the next time he said this to another student he would be suspended.

I can tell you that this was a new one for us. I was a little disturbed by the administrator's remarks. But Nick assured me that he could handle it and because he wasn't suspended, there was no need for me to get involved. My only concern was that he acted respectfully toward the other student. I definitely wasn't upset that he told her there are only two genders.

For all of us that are over the age of fifteen who grew up thinking that there are only two genders, we have to wonder—what in the world is going on? Why, when for centuries, societies all over the world have endorsed the idea that there are only two categories in the gender column—male and female—are we being told that this is no longer the case?

A brief disclaimer at this point: I realize that there are abnormalities, and specific cases where babies have been born with both sets of sex organs, or neither. That happens in 1 out of 2,000 births, or .02% of the general population. Because we live in a fallen world, I'm not denying that it happens or that there are exceptions to the rule. But what I am addressing is the claim that the rules have changed.

The good news is that the biological facts have not changed: baby boys and baby girls continue to be born every day; the bad news is the way that we view these facts has changed.

In recent years there has been an effort to separate gender from biological sex. There is a belief in our current culture that sexual orientation is not dictated by the biological sex we were assigned at birth.

This belief by many is so firmly held that even the implication that men and women are different and distinct from each other—the natural order outlined in Genesis 1—is considered offensive. During the Supreme Court confirmation hearing of Amy Coney Barrett in October of 2020, Ms. Barrett drew criticism from the LGBTQ community by using the phrase "sexual preference" in response to a question from the Senate Judiciary Committee.

Senator Mazie Hirono, D-Hawaii, chastised Barrett for using the phrase because it suggests that sexual orientation is a choice. "Sexual orientation is a normal expression of human sexuality," Senator Hirono responded.[49]

Within days of this exchange, Merriam-Webster changed the definition of the term "sexual preference" in its on-line dictionary to include that it is considered "offensive" to suggest that a person can choose who they are sexually attracted to.[50]

Boys will be...Girls?

The idea that sex is different than gender is not only unsubstantiated, but also dangerous.

In an interview with Dr. Michelle Cretella, President of the American College of Pediatricians, she explained that "biological sex is not assigned, it is determined at conception by our DNA, stamped into every cell of our bodies. Human sexuality is binary. Either you have a Y chromosome and develop into a male, or you don't, and you will develop into a female. There are at least 6,500 genetic differences between men and women. Hormones and surgery cannot and do not change this."[51]

Dr. Cretella has received death threats from activists asserting her claim that biological sex as determined at conception is "hate speech."

Why, then, does there appear to be so much gray area if the facts haven't changed? We're seeing an entire cultural movement that no longer believes that an individual's biological composition dictates their gender.

Universities have developed entire degree programs around the study of theories surrounding human sexuality. There are words being disseminated throughout our culture that didn't exist ten years ago. When I conducted an internet search for the word GENDER, the following information appeared.

- Gender Studies
  Gender studies is a field for interdisciplinary study devoted to gender identity and gendered representation as central categories of analysis. This field includes women's studies, men's studies, and queer studies.

- Gender Dysphoria
  Gender dysphoria involves a conflict between a person›s physical or assigned gender and the gender with which he/she/they identify. People with gender dysphoria may be very uncomfortable with the gender they were assigned, sometimes described as being uncomfortable with their body (particularly developments during puberty) or being uncomfortable with the expected roles of their assigned gender.

- Gender Ambiguity
  Gender ambiguity deals with having the freedom to choose, manipulate, and create a personal niche within any defined socially constructed code of conduct; while gender fluidity is outlawing all the rules of cultural gender assignment. It does not accept the prevalence of the two rigidly defined genders being "man" and "woman."[52]

I hesitated to print this chapter because I know my information will be outdated before the ink even dries on the page.

There is no consensus—even among those who deny that there are only two genders—on how many there really are. For example, when researching genders, I found articles claiming there were 33, 52, 58, and 64 different genders. In fact, one article entitled "Complete List of All Genders" listed forty-seven starting with the letter A![53]

I've listed just a few to give you an idea:

- Affectugender – A gender affected by mood swings
- Agender – Having no gender or a lack of gender identity
- Ambonec – Identifying as both man and woman, yet neither at the same time
- Angenital – A desire to be without primary sexual characteristics, without necessarily being genderless[54]

As a believer in Jesus Christ, I am compelled to acknowledge the truth expressed in Genesis 1:26–27: God created humanity as male and female. The Bible is very clear on this and biology hasn't changed.

It's not an accident that God stated the obvious in the creation account. He knew in his infinite wisdom that a time was coming when the natural order which was established through creation would be challenged. If you look at what is happening in America, every single foundational truth is under scrutiny. Ideas widely accepted in every country and culture throughout history are now being brought into question. For example, it wasn't that long ago that marriage between a man and a woman was regarded as sacred, babies were born as boys or girls, and murder was punishable by law.

There's a "new normal" invading our society in post-postmodern America: no idea—regardless of how basic or simple—can be assumed as right, and every opinion is viewed as equal. What we are witnessing is the expression of a different worldview.

However, not all worldviews are created equal. There are consequences to disregarding natural order.

In 2010, President Barack Obama enacted the Affordable Care Act. This legislation redefined "sex" to include "gender identity" for the purposes of nondiscrimination.[55] This ruling had unintended outcomes. For example, a biological woman visited a hospital's ER complaining of abdominal pain. Because she identified as a man, doctors were required to medically treat her according to her gender identify rather than biological sex.

The woman, who didn't realize she was pregnant, ended up delivering a stillborn child as a result of the treatment she received.[56]

As an extension of this legislation, Obama later issued guidance to public schools to make all bathrooms and locker rooms transgender. If school districts disregarded this mandate, they could face a loss of federal funding.[57] This policy exposed students—primarily girls—to sexual abuse and exploitation.

In 2017, the Trump Administration reversed the Obama-era regulation that redefined "sex," citing it as unconstitutional and a violation of the 1993 Religious Freedom Restoration Act.[58]

Although former President Obama and others fought for transgender rights, the truth regarding these policies and protections is rising to the surface. John Hopkins University, the institution that pioneered gender-reassignment surgeries, abruptly halted this surgical procedure after a survey concluded that the sex-change surgery did not improve an individual's quality of life, and offered "no advantage in terms of social rehabilitation."[59]

Eventually the surgeries were resumed after pressure from the LGBTQ community, but Psychiatrist Paul McHugh, the hospital's chief of psychiatry for over twenty-five years, still believes that being transgender is a psychological, not biological problem.[60]

A disturbing article published in 2018 discussed how transgender patients at the Oregon Health and Science University complained that their sex-change surgeries were botched. Many of these patients suffered mutilation at the hands of the doctor. As the writer states, "The doctor basically used a bunch of trans gender people to experiment on and gain experience without being properly trained."[61]

The tragic truth is that any attempt to override the natural order which God established at creation results in the weaker, vulnerable segments of a society being exploited by those more powerful. In the same way that unborn children—particularly minorities—are exploited by politicians who fear political backlash, so are confused, socially disenfranchised youth. They are being told that it's perfectly normal to be subjected to new, untested drug treatments and surgeries.

During an election town hall, Democratic presidential candidate Joe Biden suggested that children as young as eight-years-old should be allowed to decide if they want to become transgender. He added that there should be no discrimination against a child who makes this choice. "There is no reason to suggest that there should be any right denied your daughter...that your other daughter has a right to be and do."[62]

Biden's comments drew sharp criticism from observers on Twitter. One commenter replied, "Sure, because any parent who has sat there and listened to their kids change their minds on Halloween costumes 10 times in a month thinks this is a good idea."[63]

Another pointed example of how weaker individuals are being exploited by the stronger can be seen in how transgender females (individuals who have transitioned from male to female) are cleaning up in girls' sports. In February of 2019, transgender females competed—and won—the Girls' State Track Championship in Connecticut.[64] In fact, both first and second place were awarded to biological males competing as females. Connecticut is one of 17 states to allow transgender high school athletes to compete without restrictions.

Biology, not to mention common sense, tells us that males are physically stronger and are generally superior athletically to girls. Everyone understands this. When the US Women's Soccer team is looking for a competitive scrimmage leading up to the Olympics, they don't play the US Men's Team. Instead, they scrimmage a selected boy's high school team because they match up more competitively with the women's team. These talented women at the peak of their athletic careers understand that their male counterparts are naturally stronger and faster.

Allowing biological males to compete as girls against other girls could bring about the end of girls' sports.

Sex and Marriage

Individual governments can make laws acknowledging different unions—such as allowing same-sex marriage—but this doesn't change the natural order the Creator of the universe set in place.

The reason the Bible contains very strong warnings against ALL sexual sins, including promiscuity and extra-marital affairs, is because these are regarded as committing crimes against our own body. God has assigned you owner-ship of your physical body and wants you to take care of it.

Run from sexual sin! No other sin so clearly affects the body as this one does. For sexual immorality is a sin against your own body. Don't you realize that your body is the temple of the Holy Spirit, who lives in you and was given to you by God? You do not belong to yourself, for God bought you with a high price. So you must honor God with your body (1 Corinthians 6:18–20).

As the mastermind behind all of creation, God wrote the owner's guide for our life and existence on earth. Think of it as the manufacturer's instructions that you receive any time you purchase a car, appliance, or other product. Likewise, the Bible contains specific instructions on how to care for our physical bodies in order to receive the great-est return on our investment. The need for proper nutrition and exercise are also part of how God designed our bodies for maximum performance.

God created sex to be enjoyed and respected between one man and one woman in an exclusive, committed relationship within the boundaries of marriage. Any other sex acts are considered an abuse and can bring on consequences to our physical and emotional state. Sexually transmitted diseases, broken and/or abusive relationships, unwanted pregnancies, and even depression in certain cases could be considered some of the repercussions resulting from misuses of human sexuality.

Just as with any owner's guide, there is a strong warning against using a product in any manner other than originally intended. Doing so can void the manufacturer's warranty. In this case, coloring outside the lines when it comes to sex can jeopardize our ability to live healthy lives and enjoy fulfilling, long-lasting relationships. Heterosexual marriage relationships aren't always perfect by any stretch of the imagination. However, statistically speaking they last significantly longer and participants report higher levels of satisfaction than among homosexual partners.

The Wrap-Up

God created men and women distinctly and separate from each other at the beginning of time. Marriage between one man and one woman is one of the earliest institutions known to man and it has been recognized throughout history in every nation and every culture. This idea remains intact today. We can't gloss over the truth simply because the biblical viewpoint is unpopular and politically incorrect in our current culture.

Attempting to redefine sexuality is presumptuous and dangerous. This can lead to individuals becoming angry, confused, and exploited. In the words of conservative commentator, Tucker Carlson:

> *Gender is not a social construct; it is a biological reality. Men and women are inherently different; they are not interchangeable. Pretending otherwise is not just absurd and anti-science it is also a sure-fire way to make healthy relationships impossible, families fail and a society collapse.*[65]

Please understand—God does not hate gay people, transgenders, nor any other arbitrarily named group of individuals. Instead, God proves over and over again that He loves all individuals, for He created them in his own likeness. He goes to great lengths and personal pain to deliver and restore each one. The Creator of the universe and author of the human race doesn't judge us by the labels we wear, but by our motives, attitudes, and actions.

Likewise, our response as human beings, and especially as Christians, should be kindness and compassion. We are all sinful, broken people. We can be tolerant and respectful of everyone, even when we don't agree with their choices.

What God is really saying when He says "no" is—don't do it, because this will hurt you. God—in his ultimate wisdom—wants us to enjoy long-lasting, fulfilling relationships. He wants to protect us from unnecessary pain.

Discussion Guide

Chapter 4: Gender Reveal

The purpose of this section is to help you facilitate a meaningful discussion surrounding the material in this chapter.

1. Can you summarize the main idea of this chapter?

2. What did Dr. Cretella, President of American College of Pediatricians, mean when she said "human sexuality is binary"?

3. If you are a parent, what concerns would you have with allowing—by law—a child as young as eight years old decide if they wanted to pursue a sex change?

4. Does your state allow biological males identifying as females to compete as girls in sports? Would you be for or against your state legalizing this policy?

5. What is our responsibility as Christians toward those who hold different views about human sexuality?

6. What should be our responsibility as Christians to get involved with policy decisions, such as the ones mentioned in this chapter, which could directly or indirectly impact future generations?

Scriptures to read and discuss:

- Matthew 19:4
- 1 Corinthians 6:9–10
- Ephesians 5:3
- Romans 1:26–27
- Colossians 1:27
- 1 Timothy 1:9–10

5

Socialism Distancing

In February of 2015, we had the opportunity to visit Cuba. My husband and I spoke at a leadership conference to a group of over three hundred pastors in Santa Clara, central Cuba. It's a beautiful country with amazingly resilient people. We absolutely loved our time there but were heart-broken at the abject poverty we witnessed.

On our second day there, we visited a family who hosted a church in their home in a remote area. Since the government notoriously shuts down churches—often leveling them to the ground—Christians are forced to hold church in their homes. The church of this particular family consisted of ninety regular attenders on any Sunday morning. They met in their living room, an area approximately twelve-feet-by-twenty-feet!

This couple had three sons as well as another family member living with them, but I only noticed one bed—a dirty mattress sitting on the concrete floor.

Cubans are highly educated, hardworking people, even though each worker makes the equivalent of $30 per month. This is true regardless of profession. Custodians make the same amount as doctors in this country. They are not given a choice of where they go to college, or even which career they will pursue—the government tells them what they will study. Young men are forced to join the military, known as compulsory service.

The Castro brothers "sell" doctors, engineers, and other highly trained professionals to other countries to work in desolate, high crime areas where their local citizens refuse to work. The receiving country pays the Castros, not the employee or even the government. An individual can't refuse because if he does he will never work again since everyone works for the state.[66]

The citizens of Cuba do not have the ability to pursue happiness or liberty.

The socialist mantra is, "From each according to their ability, to each according to their needs." This sounds reasonable, doesn't it? Many dictators and autocrats rose to power by promising to build a utopian world where there is no struggle between economic classes, and everyone gets what they need. Karl Marx, author of the infamous *Communist Manifesto* believed that capitalism was doomed to fail, but abundance and harmony were achievable if communities would commit to sharing resources and denounce private ownership.[67]

Many across the world took the bait. At one point in the late 1970s, sixty percent of people worldwide were under socialist governments.

Social Experiments

There's a long list of failed experiments with socialism. The widespread devastation caused by World War II left many countries scrambling for new solutions. European colonialism—the practice of Great Britain and other wealthy countries exerting political and military authority over many smaller territories in order to exploit them for cheap labor and abundant natural resources—had failed. Countries previously controlled by Great Britain or other nations were finally establishing their independence.

Future leaders fighting to gain power across the world saw socialism—in one form or another—as a shortcut to economic prosperity for their struggling countries. If the government controlled all means of production, they reasoned, wealth could be redistributed evenly so that everyone would benefit. This proved to be an illusion in every case.

Some of these experiments began quite innocently. Julius Nyerere in Tanzania, East Africa, sincerely believed that he could rebuild the country and increase its wealth. But instead of creating economic prosperity through a market economy, Nyerere ordered all citizens to abandon their private property and move to collective farms where the government would redistribute the spoils. Instead of generating wealth, these policies proved to be very inefficient and led to more bureaucracy.

The people, now pushed to the brink of starvation, rebelled and burned down the villages.

Nyerere's flawed logic had tragic consequences: massive food and gasoline shortages. Government corruption exploded because it now held all the power. Instead of creating prosperity, his actions led to wide-scale starvation and despair.[68]

Other emerging leaders were not as naïve. Their promise to create a utopian society was nothing more than an elaborate and deliberate grab for power. Mao Zedong in China, for example, pledged his countrymen the one thing they all wanted: life-long, basic economic security. The Chinese people soon came to realize the cost was submission. The Chinese government controlled everything in their lives, including who they married and how many children they had. Even the clothes they wore and the books they read were dictated by the government.[69]

Many brutal dictators successfully sold this dream of *peace on earth*, only to devastate their country's economy, oppress their people ruthlessly, and crush any opposition. Vladimir Lenin promised Russia "Peace, Bread, and Land" in 1918; Jawaharlal Nehru promised India the end of poverty in 1947; Mao Zedong promised China there would be open debate in 1956;[70] Fidel Castro promised Cuba prosperity in 1960; and Hugo Chávez promised Venezuela universal healthcare in 1998.

Contrary to popular opinion, socialism and Communism are more similar than they are different, and socialism leads to Communism more often than it does not. Regardless of the intention or methods, one thing is clear from history: every single experiment with variations of socialism has resulted in epic failure and untold human suffering.

Venezuela was once Latin America's richest country and one of its longest-running democracies. Hugo Chávez rose to power by promising the poorest citizens of his country that the government would take care of them, provide free healthcare, and lift them out of poverty. His plan was to redistribute Venezuela's great wealth, primarily from its vast natural resources. The lower class believed him and he was overwhelmingly elected in 1998.

It appeared to work for a time—until oil prices plummeted. The government had abolished private industry and took over oil production. Under the new regime, production from oil refineries which had the capacity to produce 1.3 million barrels per day fell to 7,000 barrels per day. This was due to going years without maintenance and the breakdown of production systems.[71] Government can never run businesses as efficiently as private industry.

A university study in 2017 testified that Venezuelans reported losing an average of twenty-four pounds of body weight from starvation[72] in one year after their government oversaw the destruction of its democracy and economy, plunging much of the country into desperate poverty.[73]

Poverty, I've observed, is a political construct. Governments control the economic wellbeing of their citizens in the same way that a puppet master moves the strings on the marionette.

Democratic Socialism

This same promise of social utopia has been repackaged and sold in America as democratic socialism. Alexandria Ocasio-Cortez, New York Congresswoman, promised single-payer healthcare, tuition-free public colleges, and a guaranteed living wage to all Americans in an interview with Business Insider in March of 2019.[74]

I feel like I've seen this movie before, and it doesn't end well.

Let's not forget that we already have a prototype of socialized medicine in the United States. It's called the VA. The Veterans Health Administration has the largest integrated health care system in the United States. Its 1,243 health care facilities, including 172 VA Medical Centers and 1,0622 outpatient sites serve 9 million Veterans each year.[75]

The CBS hit drama *Seal Team* aired an episode in April of 2019 exposing the VA system. This episode, appropriately named "Medicate and Isolate," highlights the struggle of a veteran by the name of Brett Swann who was seeking help for his war injuries.[76] Finally, after years of failing to hold down a job and losing every important relationship in his life, Brett recognizes that he suffered a traumatic brain injury during one of his many deployments.

He schedules another appointment at the VA, fully knowing what to expect. The show captures the long waiting lines, poor service, and hopelessness of many of the veterans waiting to be seen. After sitting in the waiting room for over eight hours, the receptionist tries to reschedule Brett's appointment—for over two months away! After being coerced by Brett's friend, the doctor eventually agrees to see him.

When Brett is finally seen, the doctor acknowledges that his symptoms definitely could have resulted from an explosion he encountered in Iraq ten years earlier. But since his injury went undiagnosed by doctors at the time of the event, the VA system rejects Brett for treatment for his brain injury. Instead, the overworked doctors and staff have no other option but to prescribe Brett with more anti-depressants.

The episode culminates when Brett—recognizing that he's out of options and hope—takes his own life in the parking lot of the VA facility. Yes, Brett is a fictional character and this is a drama series, not a documentary. However, CBS accurately captured the essence of the VA system and how it has failed some of our most faithful citizens.

The VA medical system developed after World War II granted power to the government to make healthcare decisions for our nation's Veterans. Although the system still works in many cases because of the dedicated medical professionals the government employs, the VA system has suffered several black eyes in recent years.

In 2014, a scandal involving then President Obama's mishandling of Veterans Affairs came to light. A Newsmax article disclosed how 35 veterans that year died while waiting for appointments to be seen at VA medical facilities, just in the Phoenix area. Across the country, at least another 24 veterans have died while waiting for care.[77]

Although still not perfect, the VA has turned the corner. The MISSION Act, under President Trump, took effect in June of 2019 and privatizes some care. This policy serves to give control back to Veterans to make decisions over their own healthcare.

Europe and Socialism

Many have claimed that socialism is working in Europe; however, this depends on your definition of success. There is a lot of confusion among Americans—understandably—concerning European politics.

Democratic socialists typically cite Sweden, the Nordic country in Northern Europe, as the example of where socialized medicine is successfully practiced. Sweden has a robust market economy predominantly comprised of privately-owned businesses which fund their vast social programs.[78] Sweden has also benefited from staying out of World War II and other global conflicts which would have depleted their national reserves.

In other words, capitalism funds Sweden's socialized healthcare system and other government-run programs. The government can finance these programs because the average Swede is taxed at a rate of nearly 50%.

Even though Sweden benefited initially from socialized medicine, the healthcare system has fallen behind in recent years. According to Stanley Feld M.D., FACP, MACE, "Swedes are losing interest in the concept of a socialist society. The complaint is that it is inefficient, and, in most areas, the socialistic system does not work to the benefit of the people."[79]

For example, the town of Solleftea in Northern Sweden has 20,000 residents. The only maternity ward in town was shut down in 2014 to save the government money. Since the closest maternity ward is now over 125 miles away from town, midwives offer classes on how to deliver babies in cars—a skill which has proven very useful in many instances.[80] In an article in a local paper entitled, "Sweden's Healthcare is an Embarrassment," author Johan Hjertqvist reports that waiting times in Sweden's hospitals are among the worst in Europe.[81]

The healthcare dilemma in Sweden has been exasperated in recent years by their immigration crisis. This crisis began in 2015 when over 100,000 refugees poured into the country from Syria, Afghanistan and Iraq in just one year's time seeking asylum. An additional 70,000 refugees applied for asylum in the following two years.[82]

Swedes are very angry about the flood of immigrants pouring into their country and putting a strain on the healthcare system, delaying wait times for regular citizens.[83] To make matters worse, Sweden's over-extended healthcare system is one of the most expensive systems in all of Europe. Despite the scarcity of hospital beds, long wait times, and shortage of doctors and nurses, Sweden spends 11% of its GDP on healthcare.[84]

The welfare state created by liberal immigration policies is creating an unsustainable financial crisis in Sweden. The country of 9 million citizens—slightly larger than the population of New York City—has now committed to providing care to hundreds of thousands of refugees for life. The citizens of Sweden fear the long-term political, cultural, and economic effects to their country that only time will tell.

Other countries in Europe are not faring much better. In 2013, I had the opportunity to visit Brussels, Belgium to work with an international organization aiding victims of human trafficking. Two observations I made regarding Belgians from that visit: 1) it seemed that everyone drove a black BMW sedan, and 2) although many were helpful, very few Belgians ever smiled. One of the missionaries we worked with explained that even though Belgians have everything they need to live comfortably, most are unhappy.

The Belgium government taxes incomes at 51%, we were told. Business owners aren't concerned with providing good customer service, because it won't increase their profit margin. Belgians, according to my friend, are just going through the motions because they know they can never get ahead.

Recently the people of Great Britain issued a referendum on socialism by voting in Conservative Party leader Boris Johnson in 2019. Johnson won a decisive victory by securing 43% more of the popular vote than his rival; the largest winning margin in 60 years. Johnson's opponent, the leader of the Labour Party, Jeremy Corbyn, identifies himself as a democratic socialist. The people of Great Britain rejected the radical socialist ideology when they went to the polling booths that year.[85]

As Margaret Thatcher—the Prime Minister of England and the Conservative Party leader who rescued her country's economy in 1979 after years of failed socialist policies—said, "The trouble with socialism is that you eventually run out of other people's money."[86]

The Bible and Economics

What does the Bible say about the idea of "from each according to their ability, to each according to their needs," as the socialism mantra states? Scripture tells us more than you may think.

The very nature of mankind opposes the notion that we will ever have utopia here on earth. For socialism to work properly, benevolence and serving others instead of ourselves would have to be paramount. But people are selfish by nature. Paul spends a lot of time in his letters to the churches talking about our self-centeredness as human beings and speaking to the fallout this caused in the early Christian church.

At one point, Paul addresses a problem happening in the church at Thessalonica, a city located in modern day Greece. The year was circa 51 A.D. Certain individuals had become lazy and stopped working. They depended on others in the church for support. Instead of working to provide for their own food and necessities, these people felt it was the responsibility of the church.

Paul's response? "Those unwilling to work will not get to eat."[87]

Paul wasn't trying to be cruel; he was aiming to help all members of the church thrive by being self-sufficient. He understood how devastating it could be to an organization if a few individuals carried the responsibility for many others, especially those capable of providing for themselves. He also knew that this would free up valuable resources for those who were truly in need.

If we look back even further, we see basic social and economic principles in action in very early civilizations. Abraham, the man credited with being the "father of many nations," was very wealthy: he owned property, planted crops, hired workers, accumulated possessions, and protected his assets.

It's important for us to understand that every civilized society establishes rules to protect individuals and their ability to provide for themselves and their families. Throughout history, cultures that failed on this task didn't survive.

For example, the nation of Israel exists today because its founders understood these basic principles, even thousands of years ago. After the Jews' famous escape from Egypt, recorded in the book of Exodus, Moses is tasked with establishing a new, sovereign nation. The remainder of Exodus, Leviticus, Numbers, and Deuteronomy record God's laws and instructions for this brand-new society. These books record detailed instructions, among other things, on how to build buildings, plant vineyards, and prepare supplies they will need for survival.

The Ten Commandments given to Moses on Mount Sinai outlined the rule of law for this new nation and provided a basis for all civilized societies. Worship God first and only. Respect God's name. Honor your parents who gave you life. Don't murder. Don't sleep with someone else's spouse. Don't steal. Don't lie. Don't crave your neighbor's stuff.

These commands exemplify God's natural order. When properly applied, these rules can and have benefited every individual and society known to man since the beginning of time. When these laws are disregarded, however—such as "don't murder"—the results are devastating.

The idea of socialism is unnatural. From the beginning of time, individuals have benefited from hard work, self-discipline, and honesty. They have understood the need to provide for themselves and to protect their property and possessions from those looking for the "easy way out." It's not natural to work really hard so that the profit you make can be given to others who are lazy and do nothing.

This doesn't mean, however, that we shouldn't help others. We are compelled as citizens of heaven to help orphans and widows (James 1:27), care for the poor (Proverbs 19:17), and help strangers (1 John 3:17). But, according to the Bible, this is our individual choice and we'll be rewarded for our good deeds by God.

Charlie Kirk, founder of Turning Point USA, a non-profit organization advocating for conservative principles on university campuses, was asked if Jesus was a socialist. Kirk points out that Jesus was, first and foremost, the Savior of the world—not a political activist. He also points out that our charge as Christians "starts and ends with the individual calling, not the collective calling."[88] We can't abdicate our responsibility for providing for the poor or others in need to the government or anyone else.

We'll discuss this in more detail in the next chapter, *Capital Gains.*

The Wrap-Up

Socialism always begins with the promise of utopia but leads to tyrannical rule.[89]

Even prosperous democracies such as Germany in the 1930s, Venezuela in the 1990s, and Sweden in the 2010s, can succumb to destructive policies and mismanagement which bankrupt the economy and destroy the culture.

The failure of socialism is predictable because it defies the laws of nature. People are instinctively selfish. And even though we are social beings and desire community, we all have an innate (natural) need for autonomy.

The erroneous idea that the government should own all property and distribute to all individuals evenly is an insult to our God-given intellect. To be candid, individuals never benefit from government control over the means of production or service providers, only the politicians in power.

"If socialists understood economics, they wouldn't be socialists," claimed Friedrich Von Hayek, the Nobel Prize winner in Economics in 1974.[90]

Discussion Guide

Chapter 5: Socialism Distancing

The purpose of this section is to help you facilitate a meaningful discussion surrounding the material in this chapter.

1. Can you summarize the main idea of this chapter?

2. What is promised by democratic socialists in America?

3. Do you agree or disagree with the author's assertion that the Veterans Administration is a form of socialized medicine? Does this make you more confident or less confident in socialized medicine?

4. In what ways does the government seek to become "god" in our lives under socialism?

5. Do you agree or disagree with the author's claim that socialism (i.e., the government should collect and redistribute wealth) is unnatural?

6. Who do you think should be responsible for taking care of the poor?

Scriptures to read and discuss:

*   Proverbs 10:22
*   Proverbs 12:24
*   Proverbs 13:11
*   Ecclesiastes 5:18
*   Hebrews 6:10

6

Capital Gains

Pastor Chris Griffin, a long-time family friend, told me about his trip to Uzbekistan in November of 2019. Chris was part of a delegation sent by the US State Department to the predominantly Muslim country in Central Asia.

"You went *where?*" I'm not sure that I had even heard of Uzbekistan prior to that day.

Chris explained the purpose for his trip to this relatively obscure country. A new leader rose to power in Uzbekistan in 2016 after 25 years of Communist rule. The newly appointed Prime Minister, Shavkat Mirziyoyev made a bold decision to move his country toward democracy by abolishing child labor, creating tax reform, establishing free trade, and offering amnesty to some political prisoners.[91] This verdict took many by surprise, including his own countrymen.

No one from the United States suspected the sudden move away from Communism toward democracy either. The Clinton Administration had designated Uzbekistan as a CPC or Country of Particular Concern in 1998 because of their flagrant human rights violations.[92]

Mirziyoyev, however, wanted to chart a fresh course for the Uzbeki people and enlisted the help of the US government. He and his administration invited this diverse group of ministers and lawyers from the United States to attend a forum focusing on religious liberty and increasing personal freedoms. This new Prime Minister took seriously his commitment to increase human rights and allow diversity of thought and religious expression by showing his commitment to changing the laws.

The country's strategic placement in the region showed great potential for commerce, and the new leadership wanted to capitalize on this. While he was there, Chris noticed some glimmers of hope—new construction projects and nice hotels—but he also noticed a lot of baggage left over from years of communist rule. Despite the prime minister's commitment to improving human rights, Uzbekistan still has over one million modern slaves trapped in the cotton industry, mostly women and children. This is over 4% of the country's population. Also, homosexuality is still illegal there and offenders could be fined or sent to prison.

Remarkably, with the enormous challenges the nation still faced, the quest for religious freedom was at the top of their list! The predominantly Sunni Muslim country technically allowed other religions to co-exist, but never encouraged it. They commonly used legislative means, such as making the application process cumbersome, to discourage diversity. Uzbeki leadership demonstrated their commitment to progress by streamlining the application process and enabling religious organizations to purchase their own property.

Senator Safoev, first Deputy Chairman of the Senate, made this amazing declaration during one of the meetings with the US delegation, *"You must have free hearts to have free minds, and you must have free minds to have free markets."* The new administration recognized the inexplicable connection between religious freedom, property rights, capitalism, and prosperity.

In August of 2020, Chris received word that the very first Evangelical Church in Uzbekistan officially made it on the books after their paperwork was approved.[93]

Capitalism has created more wealth and opportunity worldwide than any other economic system throughout history. According to Brett Bair in his video series "The Unauthorized History of Socialism," capitalism has been responsible for lifting over a billion people out of poverty.[94]

The United States of America—under capitalism—has held the reputation of the largest economy in the world since 1871. The United States holds a 23.6% share (nearly a fourth) of the world's economy with an annual Gross Domestic Product (GDP) of $21.44 trillion. The bottom 173 countries combined comprise less than one-fourth of the total global economy.[95]

An individual who makes just $34,000 annual income is in the top 1% of the richest people in the world, and half of the world's wealthiest individuals live in the United States![96]

Often citizens of other countries have the notion that ALL Americans are wealthy. Many developing countries welcome American tourists; some even beg for them to come to their country. I can personally attest to this truth, having traveled to Uganda, Rwanda, Cuba, and the Dominican Republic.

Our kids would concur with this, too. Our older two children have deployed to Kuwait, Afghanistan, Guam, and Qatar at various times while enlisted in the Air Force, and our youngest visited Myanmar with his youth group. They have visited some of the poorest regions in the world. Even in countries that have leadership that hate us, everyone wants what Americans have. It seems they know that— more than any other country—Americans are willing to share their wealth.

According to a MarketWatch article, "The United States is the No. 1 most generous country in the world for the last decade."[97] Americans are some of the most charitable individuals in the world, giving more than $427 billion in 2018 to US charities alone, to say nothing of charities worldwide providing relief to children and adults of impoverished countries. It's possible that this number is actually much higher since many have stopped claiming tax deductions for their charitable donations after the 2017 tax overhaul.[98]

Three reasons pointing to why capitalism is the superior economic system include: incentive, innovation, and competition, according to Mike Huckabee in his book *The Three C's That Made America Great* (p. 123). We'll explore these below.

Incentive: Unlike socialism, Communism, and other similar systems, capitalism rewards individuals for hard work. Other systems create dependence and penalize motivation. Without the motivation to improve, individuals, companies, teams, and even governments can become complacent.

My first experience coaching soccer came in my late 20s when I was the assistant coach for a boys' middle school team. In soccer, only 11 players are on the field at the same time and we had a roster of 33 players! This is every coach's nightmare. The team wasn't very good and I soon came to understand why.

The head coach's philosophy was that everyone got equal playing time. The players loved the idea that everyone had the same chance to play... at first.

Every game, regardless of our competition, resulted in a similar outcome. We would be competitive for the first 20 minutes, until the substitutions began. He would take out our top guys and sub in less skilled players. By the third round of substitutions, we had people on the field who had never played soccer before. They only joined the team to get out of their 8th period classes. We lost every game that year.

Halfway through the season Ben, our star player—the only one who could score—quit the team. He felt it made more sense to focus his energy on his Olympic Development team. With our team, he was not rewarded with more playing time for his skill or effort. Instead, the weakest players on the team were incentivized to stay without any expectations from them.

The next year I got my own team and never used that system again. The players who had invested the most time and intensity in developing their skills and getting in shape received the most playing time. Everyone had an opportunity to play but had to first prove their commitment to help the team.

Innovation: Capitalism rewards innovation, but socialism suppresses it. During the 2020 economic shutdown resulting from the COVID-19 pandemic, for example, innovation proved to be king. There was still profit to be made, but companies and individuals had to show ingenuity in order to overcome the drastic economic downturn due to restrictions.

Restaurants and the service industry were hit particularly hard during this time. Many closed their doors permanently. Others, however, thrived under the adversity. Sebastian Oveysi, Iranian-born chef and co-owner of Amoo's in Washington, DC, devised another plan when sales plummeted 65 percent at the beginning of the pandemic.

"Our family survived a revolution and the extremism that followed it. Then we escaped through a border covered in mines," said Oveysi. "We can get through a pandemic, too."[99] The business purchased a food truck and posted the truck's adventures on social media. Homeowners associations throughout the area took notice and now he has bookings every week.

Necker's Toyland, a toy store in Simsbury, Connecticut, that's been in business since 1948, also had to get creative. Sales at their retail stores tanked during the lockdowns, for obvious reasons. They began offering a FaceTime browsing option, virtually walking kids around the store, so they can pick out something that would keep them busy during the quarantine.[100]

Competition: Competition is a key reason why capitalism works. Competition forces down prices and creates accountability. When there is no competition—as in the case of major retailer Amazon and electronics lynchpin Apple—consumers lose their ability to control the market. Instead, the companies are in charge: they can hike prices, be careless with quality, and buy out prospective competition.

Competition benefits everyone. Competing companies benefit from increased marketing which exponentially expands consumer exposure. Bottled water is a prime example of an industry benefiting from product awareness. Even though the company Poland Spring began selling bottled water to summer visitors of their Maine resort in 1845, and Perrier mineral water began advertising in popular American magazines in 1910,[101] it wasn't until later in the twentieth century that bottled water became relevant. In the 1990s various US companies such as Deer Park, Nestle Pure Life, Arrowhead, Niagara, Smartwater, and others began producing bottled water, creating more attention and demand for the product.

The main reason many government agencies are notorious for poor service is because of the lack of competition. The Disney movie *Zootopia* released in 2015 comically portrays this stereotype. Judy Hopps, the bunny cop trying to solve a case, is delayed when she needs assistance at the Department of Motor Vehicles. Much to her dismay, all the employees at the DMV are sloths! (Sloths are the notoriously slow-moving mammals from South America who have become synonymous with the idea of being idle and lazy.) Needless to say, service at the DMV was extremely slow that day.

The school system in America has also fallen into this trap. The lack of competition in public schools has produced disastrous results, particularly in low income areas. According to the 2019 Nation's Report Card, only slightly more than one-third of eighth graders are proficient in reading.[102] The high spot of the report is that forty percent of fourth graders are proficient in math. Sadly, the good news equates to less than half of all ten-year-olds having advanced math skills.

Some areas of the country scored worse than others. Within the Baltimore City Public Schools, only thirteen percent of fourth graders tested above proficiency in reading.[103] Another alarming statistic points to the fact that nine-out-of-ten black boys in Baltimore City can't read at their current grade level. That means that in this region 90% of black men grow up without basic reading skills. Also, in over a dozen high schools across the district, not a single student tested proficient in math.[104]

To be clear, I have great respect for teachers. I personally know many, many exceptional professionals in this field. The problem isn't our teachers, it's the bureaucracy which eliminates competition and breeds complacency, particularly in minority neighborhoods.

For this reason, the Trump Administration and many of its supporters have declared School Choice—the ability of parents to use their own tax dollars to send their children to the school of their choosing—the Civil Rights issue of our time. Kim Klacik, the Republican candidate for Maryland's 7th District, ran her campaign based on the platform of how school choice seeks to break the "school-to-prison-pipeline" fueled by tragically ineffective schools in many inner cities.[105]

Proponents of school choice are confident this policy would force underperforming schools to improve by introducing competition within the public school system. When multiple schools are competing for the same students, schools will need to improve methods and results in order to stay viable.

The Downside of Capitalism

If you were to ask ten people the downside of capitalism, most likely nine of them would say greed.

It's true; there are many greedy people in our capitalistic society. Wealthy hedge-fund investors on Wall Street come to mind. Bernie Madoff, former chairman of the NASDAQ (National Association of Securities Dealers Automated Quotations) stock market became notorious for operating the largest Ponzi scheme in history. A Ponzi scheme is an elaborate financial scam where early investors are repaid with money received from later investors, not actual investment income.[106]

Madoff exploited his relationships with wealthy businessmen in New York and Florida in order to attract more investors. When he paid out handsome dividends (by using other people's money), these influential individuals encouraged their friends to invest with him, also. Madoff was indicted in 2009 when he plead guilty to fraud, money laundering, and other crimes. He is still serving his sentence in federal prison.

To say that capitalism is fueled by greed, however, is not substantiated.

Jay W. Richards dispels this myth in his book, *Money, Greed and God* (HarperOne, 2009). There is a difference between selfishness and self-interest, according to Richards. Capitalism is driven by self-interest because it seeks mutually beneficial transactions. For example, if you are a real estate agent you look to sell to people who need what you're offering—a home. Free markets exist because some have needs and others have products/services to fulfill those needs. Looking out for our self-interests isn't selfish, it's necessary for survival.

There's plenty of room for corruption in any economic system, whether it be socialism, capitalism, or any variation in between. The difference lies in who controls the power.

In capitalism, for example, the consumer is in control. Individuals have the option of choosing the car they will purchase, the house they will buy, the college they will attend, and the amount of savings they will invest. Unfortunately, unsuspecting consumers can be exploited by greedy, unscrupulous actors into investing in products or services which yield less than optimal returns.

Everywhere you look, powerful corporations are inventing ways to manipulate the customer. Advertisers invest millions to persuade and even coerce us. Most of us have been caught up at one time or another—and to one degree or another—by their deceptive plots. But, at the end of the day, the consumer is still in charge.

In socialism, however, the government is in power. Those who hold political power make all the decisions, as we discussed last chapter. This is why socialized medicine is not the answer. Yes, you may not have to pay for your doctor's visits, but a government bureaucrat decides which doctor you will see, when you will see them, what procedures you are authorized to have, and which doctor will operate. You may not get a bill in the mail, but you have lost control over your own care.

Capitalism isn't perfect, but it's worlds better than any other economic system.

Wealth and Poverty

The idea that capitalism contributes to poverty is another myth. Compelling evidence proves that the opposite is true.

The country of Venezuela was once a thriving democracy, as discussed in Chapter 5. In 1989, it's estimated that only 25% of households in the country were living below the poverty line. In 2017, however—after the deployment of socialistic policies designed to redistribute wealth took effect—87% of households were reported to be living in poverty.

There are a few reasons why countries with thriving market economies—where capitalism is at work—have fewer citizens below the poverty line than countries where the government controls all means of production. The first reason why the poorest individuals in a society do better under a thriving economy can be explained using "Reagonomics." President Ronald Reagan, when outlining his plan for the Economic Recovery Tax Act of 1981,[107] demonstrated how all members of society benefit from economic growth because those with the greatest resources can create the greatest opportunities. Prospects for employment at all levels of the salary scale improve under a healthy economy.

In a speech given in 1963, President John F. Kennedy explained the idea that general prosperity benefits the welfare of the individual this way: "As they saw on my own Cape Cod, a rising tide lifts all the boats."[108]

The second reason why an individual benefits in a society where the wealthiest members are prospering is the fact that those who benefit the most from capitalism tend to be the most generous.[109] As noted earlier in this chapter, America is the most charitable nation year after year. It's a widely accepted truth that Christian churches in America, and their members, have done more for the poor and underserved than any other group in the world. Soup kitchens, food pantries, homeless shelters, after school programs, playgrounds and recreation centers, services to train and integrate intellectually challenged youth and adults represent just a few of the benefits private, nonprofit groups provide here in the United States.

Capitalists aren't opposed to the redistribution of wealth. We just want to distribute our own fortune. We know that we are much more efficient at it than the government.

According to Jim Garlow in his book *Well Versed*, "Care for the poor is so close to the heart of God that He placed the role with the people of God. Apparently, He knew the government could not handle it properly."

The Bible and Economics (Part II)

In the last chapter we discussed the economics of the natural order God set in place at creation. From the beginning of time we see individuals working with their hands to plant crops, raise livestock, and sew clothes. They hired workers and protected their assets. The very fact that one of the Ten Commandments is "Do not steal" assumes that individuals own things. If the Israelite community was communal (they shared possessions) there would be no need to outlaw theft, because no one would have personal rights to anything.

Socialism always fails because it is not natural. It goes against the God-given desire to work and be productive in order to provide for yourself and family. Additionally, socialism doesn't align with our innate desire for autonomy.

In this era of participation trophies and entitlement, the Parable of the Talents found in Matthew 25 doesn't seem to make much sense to us. Many are perplexed by the idea that the man in the story doesn't treat everyone "equally." Allow me to summarize the story...

A business owner calls together his employees for a meeting. He's going out of town, so he puts different individuals in charge of his assets. He makes this determination based on each individual's ability: his star employee receives five talents, his two deputy assistants receive two talents each, and his underperforming worker only received one talent.

The first employee invests his boss' money and quickly doubles his savings from five to ten talents. The second and third employees also double their investments, ending with four talents each. The third employee was just plain lazy. Instead of investing and earning minimal interest, he hid the money and sat on it.

When the man returns to check on his assets, he finds a mixed bag of results. He's very pleased with the first three employees because they doubled profits on the money entrusted to them. But he's disappointed with the last employee—to say the least—because he didn't do anything with the one talent he had.

What happens next is most perplexing. He takes the one talent from the last employee and gives it to the *first*. If one of us were writing the story, we would probably have the business owner give two of the first employee's talents to the last guy to make things fair. Not only that, but the business owner severely chastises the last employee. In fact, the punishment is so harsh that it doesn't seem to fit the crime.

This story explains how God's economy is built on the foundation of rewarding hard work and obedience [to God]. We are given talents to use to glorify God, but these gifts also serve a practical purpose: they allow us to provide for ourselves and our families. Some are naturally gifted teachers, some are talented to work in the hospitality industry, others are skilled in the trades, many are natural "protectors" and work in public service, and others are skilled entrepreneurs. We all possess God-given talents, and there are real consequences for refusing to work in ways God has gifted us.

Capitalism *is* the natural order God set in place at creation.

The Wrap-Up

Countries all over the world with thriving economies understand the connection between religious freedom, capitalism, and prosperity. Since 1970, capitalism has lifted over a billion people out of poverty.

Americans are some of the most generous in the world. The average American Christian, in particular, has volunteered their time and donated money to any number of charities, both here and overseas. Capitalists aren't against redistributing wealth, but we want the final say in how our money is used.

Free markets benefit *everyone*, including the poorest segment of the population. It's a misnomer that capitalism increases poverty. Instead of creating more poverty, capitalism creates more prosperity at all socioeconomic levels. Citizens of countries all over the world have risen out of poverty when their governments adopt policies that promote capitalism.

Deuteronomy 8:18 (ESV) says, "You shall remember the Lord your God, for <u>it is he who gives you power to get wealth</u>, that he may confirm his covenant that he swore to your fathers, as it is this day."

God, in his sovereignty, wants us to understand how to access the greatest capital gains.

Discussion Guide

Chapter 6: Capital Gains

The purpose of this section is to help you facilitate a meaningful discussion surrounding the material in this chapter.

1. Can you summarize the main idea of this chapter?

2. Why do you think there is a connect between religious prosperity, property rights, capitalism, and prosperity?

3. Explain in your own words why competition is so important to capitalism?

4. Do you agree or disagree with the statement that "consumers have the final authority in capitalism"? Explain your position.

5. Why do you think the owner in the parable of the talents punished the third servant (or employee) so harshly?

6. Do you agree or disagree that capitalism is an economic system that God established for mankind? Explain your position.

Scriptures to read and discuss:

- Proverbs 13:11
- 1 Timothy 6:17–19
- Matthew 6:19–21
- Deuteronomy 8:18
- Philippians 4:19
- Proverbs 24:8–9

7

Race is On

2020—The year that went through the cheese shredder.

Like many, I distinctly remember December 31, 2019. No one had any idea of the oppression, despair, and isolation that would fall on us like a heavy coat just weeks later. A global pandemic of the COVID-19 virus originated in Wuhan, China and was subsequently exported to all of the known world. Just like that, everything changed.

There is nothing you could have told me on December 31 to make me believe that eating at a restaurant, sitting at a coffee shop, casual "retail therapy," attending sporting events, or even gathering with our family for Easter were in danger of extinction, or even temporary disruption. Essentially overnight, large events like parades and baseball games, vacations, international travel, and even attending church were banned.

By early May we were all begging for 2020 to be canceled with no refunds and no returns. But we still had over six months to go.

Memorial Day approached and we felt as if some relief was in sight. The warm weather gave hope that everything would soon return to normal. And then June rolled in like hurricane. A video surfaced of a black man by the name of George Floyd with the foot of a white police officer on his neck in Minneapolis, causing protests to erupt over all the country.

These peaceful protests—guaranteed by the First Amendment of the Constitution of the United States— soon gave way to chaos, vandalism, and anarchy. Months of lockdowns exacerbated the need for people to express themselves. City after city saw unprecedented looting, burning, and destruction of businesses and personal property. Portland, Oregon; Seattle, Washington; Baltimore, MD; and Washington, DC, fared the worst.

After a week of protests and riots, something odd happened. Rather than diffusing and everyone going back to live as normal, the demonstrations intensified. Week after week protests and violence continued. Portland, Oregon, saw over 100 continual days of riots.[110] Many of the businesses burned to the ground during the unrest were owned by minorities. Clearly this was no longer about protesting the killing of an unarmed black man. The entire county seemed to be in chaos.

The unrest escalated. Calls to defund and dismantle police departments erupted across the entire country. Soon every news channel talked daily about racism and the need for "social justice" in America.

The Big Question

Is America systemically racist? That's the question. Unfortunately, many Americans are buying into this notion without even understanding what systemic racism means. My answer is yes, unfortunately there are elements of systemic racism in our county. BUT, it's not in the way you think.

The term systemic comes from the root word "system." A system of racism does not originate at retail level (with an individual). Systems are developed at the top of the pyramid with the higher positions of leadership, not the bottom.

Of course, there will always be certain individuals who act inappropriately. I don't deny individual racism exists, because it does. We all have heard about truly awful things which have been said and done to black folks and other minorities. Furthermore, I certainly don't condone it. We are all human beings created in the image of God, for whom Jesus died. But the idea that all of American society is defined by a few hateful individuals is a very different claim.

Let's look at areas of our society which are not racist first. The notion that our police institutions across the country are systematically racist is unfounded. The numbers don't support that narrative of police racism and brutality toward the black community. According to a USA Today article dated July 3, 2020, there is "no epidemic of fatal police shootings against unarmed Black Americans."[111]

The article backs its claim with the following: in 2019 only 14 unarmed black Americans were shot by police. That same year 25 white Americans were shot by police. Keep in mind that there are roughly 50 million police actions nationwide per year. Every single American—black, white, brown, or purple—has a one-in-a-million chance of being shot by the police.

Having said that, it's important to acknowledge that police officers do have a bias, but it's not against minorities. Their bias is against *criminals,* regardless of their skin color or gender. As with any profession, law enforcement tends to attract individuals with similar personality traits. A strong majority of police officers are very protective by nature. They willingly enter the field of law enforcement to serve and defend the community.

Nothing pushes the buttons of a protector quite like seeing a child who has suffered extreme neglect from a parent, or a woman being abused by her boyfriend, a teenager high on heroin needing immediate intervention to survive, or finding a dead body of a homeless man. Officers are continually forced to make complex, fast-paced, ambiguous decisions with minimal information.[112] The consistent exposure to these traumatic situations can affect an officer's mental health. Many studies have come out recently showing the connection between the continual exposure to trauma and an officer's ability to make split-second decisions.

Additionally, it's important to understand that law enforcement by nature is reactive, not proactive. Police officers don't make the laws, they just enforce them. There are no laws on the books presently which discriminate against individuals based on their ethnicity. To say that officers intentionally target minorities shows a misunderstanding of how the law works.

Yes, there are those who are racist within the ranks as with any profession or group of individuals. But the .001% of the bad apples aren't the root cause of the backlash against the police community. By now, many are beginning to recognize that the attacks on law enforcement are a smoke screen concealing the real problem, which we'll see in the next chapter.

Systemic racism also implies that minorities are denied the ability to thrive in America. This simply is not true. Ironically, professional athletes and Hollywood elites are typically the first ones to lecture on the subject of the oppression of minorities, and yet nowhere in America do we find more wealthy, successful black and brown individuals than in these two demographics!

One look at Forbes Magazine "Highest-Paid Athletes of 2020" confirms the truth that ethnicity is not a key determining factor in one's success in the field of athletics.[113] In fact, the sport these athletes compete in has more impact on their earnings than their race. Basketball players in the top 100 paid athletes, for example, cumulatively earned $1.2 billion, while tennis players on this list collectively made $245 million.

The notion that the average white Caucasian in America is racist is also unfounded. One of the greatest evidences of this is "Just Sam," a poor, young black woman from the Frederick Douglass Houses in Harlem, New York City who used to sing in the subways to pay the bills. She won *American Idol* in 2020. This highly rated singing competition is a television series that decides its finalists based on nationwide audience voting. Just Sam was voted the number one finalist by millions of American Idol fans across the country.

Our democratic system of governance is the only one on the planet which acknowledges every human being is created equal in the sight of God and has the opportunity to pursue happiness. Our Constitution guarantees equal opportunity, but not equal outcomes.

Galatians 3:28 says, "There is no longer Jew or Gentile, slave or free, male and female. For you are all one in Christ Jesus." The Bible makes it clear that God does not play favorites. He sent his only Son to die for our sins so that ALL may have eternal life.

Divided We Stand

Remarkably, the great divide between races seems to have reappeared lately. Looking back as recently at 2016, the discussion about racial tensions seemed to be fading. Morgan Freeman, famous for his roles in *The Shawshank Redemption* and *Bruce Almighty* commented on the ridiculousness of Black History Month in an interview with Mike Wallace on CBS' *60 Minutes*.[114] During the 2008 interview, Freeman also said that the best way to end racism is to stop talking about it.

During a 2014 interview with CNN's Don Lemon, Freeman rejected the idea that being born Black in America was an obstacle. "I don't think wealth and genetics have anything to do with each other, actually," the 80-year-old Freeman said. "Put your mind to what you want to do and go from there."[115]

Even Whoopie Goldberg, host on The View, commented in 2016 that the Academy Awards "can't be that racist because she once won a prized trophy."[116] She was one of many black celebrities who denied claims of racial bias in the article.

Fast forward to 2020. Every news network is discussing racial issues, every day. An exacerbated race war has seemingly appeared out of nowhere.

Back in the Day

There was a time when American society was "systemically racist." Even though slavery was officially abolished on September 22, 1863, by President Abraham Lincoln's Emancipation Proclamation, the fight was far from over. Factions within our government continued to persecute persons of color and systematically discriminate against them for decades. These laws were intended to marginalize African Americans by denying them the ability to hold jobs, receive an education, and vote.[117] This marks a dark time in our history.

Laws were presented and passed by individual Southern states—later known as Jim Crow Laws—beginning in the late 1870s requiring the separation of whites from "persons of color" on public transportation and in schools.[118] These principles were extended to theaters, parks, restaurants, and even cemeteries to avoid any appearance that blacks and whites were equal.

In 1896, a landmark case was tried before the United States Supreme Court. *Plessy v. Ferguson* involved the plaintiff Homer Plessy contending that his constitutional rights were being violated when he was ordered to move to the train car "for blacks." Plessy's argument was denied and segregation was upheld.[119] The *Plessy v. Ferguson* case is significant because it began the "separate-but-equal" doctrine, alleging that separate schools and transportation for blacks was legal as long as they were equal.

Finally, in 1954, the Supreme Court overturned the first legislation that kept communities segregated. In the *Brown v. Board of Education of Topeka* case the Supreme Court ruled unanimously that racial segregation of children in public schools was unconstitutional. Oliver Brown filed the suit after his daughter Linda Brown was denied entrance to Topeka's all-white elementary schools.[120]

The following year, in 1955, Rosa Parks refused to give up her seat on the bus to a white man, sparking a year-long boycott of public transportation. This boycott was led by the newly appointed pastor of Dexter Avenue Baptist church in Montgomery, Alabama—Rev. Dr. Martin Luther King, Jr. On December 20, 1956, the Supreme Court ruled on *Browder v. Gayle* and overturned racial segregation on buses, also deeming it unconstitutional.[121]

History revealed that "separate-but-equal" education, transportation, and other services were not, in fact, equal.

Since this time, the United States has made great strides toward leveling the playing field and creating opportunities for all Americans. Economic prosperity over the next few decades created an environment where nearly anyone willing to work hard and persist could succeed. Oprah Winfrey—one of the richest and most influential women in the world—for example, was born to poor, unmarried, teenaged parents. Oprah suffered repeated sexual abuse by several male relatives and friends of her mother. She eventually moved to Nashville to escape the abuse and live with her father.[122] And yet, despite the immense obstacles she faced, Oprah emerged as the first black female billionaire in America.

Many minority groups, in fact, are thriving in America. An Insider Monkey article published in March of 2018 lists the seven richest, most powerful ethnic groups in America. Russian-Americans, for example, have a median household income of $77,349. This group is superseded by Israeli-Americans at $79,736; Australian-Americans have a median household income of $81,452; Filipino-Americans with $82,389; Taiwanese-Americans at $85,566; and Jewish-Americans with a median household income of $97,500. Indian-Americans top the list with a median household income of $101,390.[123]

Policy Matters

We have a "systemic" problem in this country but it's not racism. It's poverty. We have created systems that perpetuate poverty from one generation to another.

As the Great Depression was ending, President Franklin Delano Roosevelt enacted his Social Security Act in 1935. This initiated our current welfare system by providing federal aid to the elderly, physically handicapped, and dependent mothers and children.

In 1964, Democratic President Lyndon Baines Johnson expanded this legislation by passing a series of bills as part of his "Great Society" initiative. This initiative, also known as "The War on Poverty," included a number of components:

- The Economic Opportunity Act aimed to eliminate the paradox of poverty in the midst of plenty.[124]

- The Food Stamp Act sought to use the food abundances in America to improve levels of nutrition among underserved populations.

- The Elementary and Secondary Education Act aimed to level the alleged "achievement gap" in public education.

- The Social Security Act of 1965 created Medicare and Medicaid.[125]

Although minority voters initially supported these measures, a wide gulf appeared between what under-privileged Americans hoped the legislation would achieve and what the Democrat politicians actually delivered.[126] African American communities realized the hypocrisy by the Johnson Administration and rioted the summer after the bill was passed.

The civil rights organizer Bayard Rustin said that the bill was good for ending segregation but said it did nothing to address the three major problems Negroes faced at that time: housing, jobs, and integrated schools. Because of this, Rustin commented that the frustration of these under-served communities only increased.[127]

President Ronald Reagan openly condemned the welfare system in a speech in Santa Barbara in February of 1986, denouncing it as misguided. He noted that under the current law, the federal government sets up a pregnant young woman with an apartment, medical care, clothing, and food—as long as she doesn't marry or associate with the father of her child.

We're in danger of creating a permanent culture of poverty as inescapable as any chain or bond; a second and separate America, an America of lost dreams and stunted lives... The irony is that misguided welfare programs instituted in the name of compassion have actually helped turn a shrinking problem into a national tragedy.[128]

As Reagan predicted, this legislation has attributed to an alarming phenomenon of "child mothers and absentee fathers," particularly among the poor. According to the National Vital Statistics Report published by the CDC National Center for Health Statistics, out-of-wedlock birth rates have skyrocketed since 1965. At that time, the out-of-wedlock birth rate was 25% among Blacks. This rate rose to 68% in 1991, and then escalated to 77% of black babies being born to unmarried mothers by 2015.[129]

The connection between the absence of fathers and poverty is undeniable. As noted in Chapter 2 of this book, women-only households are significantly more likely to live below the poverty line. The lack of a father in the home also greatly increases the chance a child will suffer a behavioral disorder, run away from home, be convicted of a violent offense, or end up in prison.

The "Great Society" legislation is not the only democratic policy which generated systems of poverty. Many believe that The Violent Crime and Law Enforcement Act of 1994 profoundly impacted poor communities by exacerbating the fatherlessness situation. The "Three Strikes" provision in the bill imposed mandatory life sentences for individuals with three or more felony convictions.[130] This bill sent thousands of Americans to prison for life for non-violent offenses, including offenses as minor as stealing loose change from a parked car.[131]

Even more insidious than handing out life sentences to non-violent criminals, is how the crime bill incentivized states to keep inmates jailed longer. The bill promised states $12.5 billion to build new prisons if they agreed to pass laws requiring prisoners to serve a minimum of 85% of their sentences. So, instead of focusing on rehabilitation and releasing prisoners early for good behavior, it's possible that politicians lined their own pockets by taking advantage of federal inducements.

It's understandable how this could be considered systemic racism since these policies disproportionately affect inner city minority communities. However, these policies don't affect all Black and Brown people equally, as racism implies. As discussed earlier, many minorities are thriving in America, including many who have overcome extreme poverty.

Systemic poverty is a very serious issue faced by minority communities in our country and it deserves an answer, as we'll discuss in the next chapter. Systemic *racism* in America, however, is an illusion.

During the Civil Rights Movement in the 1960s the line was clearly drawn between races, and blacks and whites were on opposite sides. The same is not true today. Many on the "social justice" side purportedly defending oppressed minorities are white, upper-middle class, young adults. Some on the opposing side saying America is not racist—but is, in fact, the land of opportunity—are themselves minorities.

Joel Patrick, a young, conservative black man from Ohio tells a story about an encounter with one of his customers. Patrick, who started his own landscaping business in his early 20s, was called by a homeowner to remove a tree that had fallen on his property. He was met at the door by the renter of the house, a middle-aged white woman employed as a professor at a local university.

When the woman opened the door and saw a young black man standing there, Patrick relays how the woman gasped and said how sorry she felt for him. He was very confused by her reaction but didn't respond. The woman continued with how terrible it must be for him, as a black man, *to be oppressed in America*. She said she teaches her students everyday about systemic racism and oppression, and she couldn't image what he was going through.

Still confused, Patrick shrugged off her remarks and continued with the appraisal, since that was his purpose for being called to the house. Later, while reflecting on the encounter, he commented to his one million viewers on Instagram how *he is not oppressed*. The woman apparently didn't understand that this so-called oppressed black man was an entrepreneur, and had driven to this call in his late model Ram 1500 TRX 4x4 Crew Cab with special-order orange paint truck which probably cost more than the house she was renting.[132]

Patrick posted this quote weeks later: "Some people take a single brick, learn to lay it, and build a business... while others take a single brick, throw it through a glass window, and complain about inequality."[133]

Why, then, does the media continue to talk about the race war in America? They belabor the conversation on how the majority is oppressing the minority, instead of holding accountable the politicians who enacted these oppressive policies which served themselves, rather than the communities entrusted to them.

In recent years it's becoming clear that the divide is between those who *think* differently, not between those who *look* differently. The real story is how individuals holding opposite political views can reach radically different conclusions when presented with the same set of facts. Unfortunately, social media and media networks are complicit with creating this divide.

Racism isn't a universal truth, it's a political construct. It's man-made. According to Dinesh D'Souza, award-winning filmmaker and best-selling author,

> *Racism is the witchcraft of the 21st century. Now, as then, it's hard to find witches. Many people haven't actually seen a witch. Yet powerful people create public hysteria and insist witches are everywhere. Some are invisible! Now, as then, it's about power and social control.*[134]

The Wrap Up

It's not our police force, laws, or other people that are preventing individuals from achieving the American dream. Rather, it is ideologies such as victimhood, entitlement, group think, and others that keep many stuck in an imaginary prison of ideas, rather than a true victim of a corrupt and intolerant system. Many of these ideologies are being pushed by political leaders and the media.

Orlando Patterson, a Jamaican-born American sociologist and professor at Harvard University said,

America is now the least racist white majority society in the world: has a better record of legal protection of minorities than any other society, white or black; [and] offers more opportunities to a greater number of black persons than any other society, including all of Africa.[135]

America is not systemically racist, but there are a few individuals from every ethnic group who spew hatred and intolerance. This tiny minority does not represent the majority of Americans, but they are receiving the largest amount of airtime on TV and social media.

In the words of Morgan Freeman, "The best way to end racism is to stop talking about it."

Poverty, however, is a systemic issue and policy matters! Legislation has a powerful impact on creating systems of both wealth and poverty. We have to demand better from our lawmakers. We'll explore in the next chapter, "Social Injustice," how the Trump Administration is actively rolling back many oppressive policies which have plagued our minority communities.

We'll also discuss in Chapter 8 how no one cares for the poor, oppressed, and marginalized more that God, and how our responsibility as believers in Jesus Christ is to do the same.

America is far from perfect, but we've made great strides to correct injustices which are contrary to our constitutional guarantees. The "American dream" is still open for business and on the menu for anyone with the will to work for it, regardless of the color of your skin.

Discussion Guide

Chapter 7: Race is On

The purpose of this section is to help you facilitate a meaningful discussion surrounding the material in this chapter.

1. Can you summarize the main idea of this chapter?

2. Do you believe that America is systemically racist? Explain your position.

3. Why do you think that some ethnic groups in America are thriving more than others?

4. Consider this: "In recent years it's becoming clear that the divide is between those who *think* differently, not between those who *look* differently." Do you agree or disagree?

5. Do you agree or disagree that race is a political construct? Defend your position.

6. Read this statement: "America is now the least racist white majority society in the world: has a better record of legal protection of minorities than any other society, white or black; [and] offers more opportunities to a greater number of black persons than any other society, including all of Africa." Why do you believe this is so?

Scriptures to read and discuss:

- Galatians 3:28
- Romans 2:11
- James 2:9
- Acts 10:34–35
- John 3:16

8

Social Injustice

The tragic death of George Floyd sent shock waves throughout the country. The call for "action for racial justice—to empower, support, and accelerate immediate solutions, as well as work toward long-term systematic transformation"[136] resonated throughout the United States.

But as time progressed, it became apparent that many of those protesting weren't looking for immediate solutions or long-term systematic transformation—they were looking for anarchy. As cities burned, one prominent political group took center stage by exploiting the chaos—Black Lives Matter (BLM).

The seemingly organic demonstrations soon gave way to "mostly peaceful protests" and/or full-on riots in many major cities in America. Arsonists set fire to retail stores, police departments, vehicles, restaurants, and even federal buildings in Portland, Seattle, New York City, Chicago, and many other cities nationwide. Pictures of decimated businesses flooded the internet. Damages from looting and vandalism totaled more than $2 billion.[137]

Overnight, these demonstrations evolved into calls to "defund the police." Within weeks, the BLM organization secured pledges from Corporate America in the amount of $1.678 billion.[138] Bank of America, for example, pledged $1 million. Nike, Sony Music Group, and Walmart pledged $100 thousand. Google, Amazon, Spotify, and Facebook—not surprisingly—also wanted a part of the action and pledged thousands of dollars.

What is Social Justice

Many individuals and organizations sincerely wanted to help those oppressed by our "systemically racist culture" in America. As a result, many people, corporations, organizations, and even churches have jumped on the social justice bandwagon.

Given recent events, many of us are contemplating what exactly is social justice and what does it accomplish? Why does it suddenly appear that after decades of prosperity for Americans from all ethnic and socioeconomic backgrounds, many now can't seem to find justice?

Consider the following definition of social justice:

Social justice is a political and philosophical theory which asserts that there are dimensions to the concept of justice beyond those embodied in the principles of civil or criminal law, economic supply and demand, or traditional moral frameworks. Social justice tends to focus more on just relations between groups within society as opposed to the justice of individual conduct or justice for individuals.

Historically and in theory, the idea of social justice is that all people should have equal access to wealth, health, well-being, justice, privileges, and opportunity regardless of their legal, political, economic, or other circumstances. In modern practice, social justice revolves around favoring or punishing different groups of the population, regardless of any given individual's choices or actions, based on value judgements regarding historical events, current conditions, and group relations. In economic terms, this often means redistribution of wealth, income, and economic opportunities from groups whom social justice advocates consider to be oppressors to those whom they consider to be the oppressed. Social justice is often associated with identity politics, socialism, and revolutionary communism.[139]

One reason social justice is so troubling is because it's not interested in solving problems and creating solutions. Rather, it's about arbitrarily "favoring and punishing different groups of the population, regardless of any given individual's choices or actions." It's the opposite of true justice; it subverts the natural order and, as a result, favors the strong while exploiting the weak. It's anti-justice in essence.

Consider the call to defund the police. Many believe this began with Floyd's death, but it didn't. Would you be surprised to learn that this movement began in the early 1900s?[140] Dr. Michael Sawyer, and associate professor at Colorado College explains that the "abolition-democracy" is all about abolishing the institutions which oppress African Americans, and has been around for over a century. The issue of "systemic police violence" and the need to eliminate funding for these institutions first appeared in articles from the editor of Crisis Magazine in 1910. [141]

This movement gained national attention in 2015 when then President Obama advocated for disbanding traditional police agencies and focusing on community policing.[142]

The reality, however, is that the notion of disbanding police departments is not supported by the minority communities who have the most to lose. According to Newsweek, 81% of Black Americans don't want less police in their neighborhoods. As much as 20% of minorities want more of a police presence in their communities.[143]

The city of Memphis, Tennessee, for example, had a crime rate in 2019 of 84-per-one- thousand residents, making it one of the ten most dangerous cities in America. Individuals have a 1-in-12 chance of being a victim of violent crime, including murder, rape, robbery, and assault. A Memphis resident also has a 1-in-15 chance of being a victim of property crime, including burglary, theft, and motor vehicle theft.[144]

Following the unrest in the summer of 2020, several major cities witnessed a sharp spike in murders, according to Forbes Magazine.[145] While some have claimed no connection between reducing funding and manpower for police departments and increases in crime, there appears to be plenty of correlation.[146] Several of the cities that began cutting funding for police departments—Chicago, New York, Philadelphia, Atlanta, and Washington D.C.—saw alarming increases in homicides.[147]

New York City, for instance, made the news when Mayor Bill de Blasio slashed $1 billion from the NYPD budget in June of 2020, and canceled a 1,200-person police recruiting class set to start the following month. The city saw a 77% increase in murder in the first six months of 2020, compared to all of 2019.[148]

Justice in Action

True justice is an action, not a philosophical ideology. As discussed in the previous chapter, decades of poor legislation oppressed many Black and Latino communities. The Three-Strikes provision in the 1994 Crime Bill increased sentences for non-violent drug offenders and made it more difficult for prisoners to be granted parole.

The Crime Bill imposed tougher sentences for those caught with crack-cocaine than those caught with powder cocaine. This disparity also seems to target minorities. According to former Rep. Keith Ellison, "Whites use cocaine, blacks use crack."[149] Whites, according to this equation, get probation, blacks get a decade behind bars.[150]

One individual caught up by the stricter sentencing guidelines resulting from the Crime Bill was Alice Marie Johnson. She was convicted in 1996 for her involvement with a crack- cocaine trafficking organization in Memphis, Tennessee. She was subsequently sentenced to life in prison without parole, even though this was her first offense. Johnson admitted her involvement with the drug trafficking organization but said that she didn't actually sell drugs or make drug deals. [151]

Johnson's case was brought to the attention of President Trump in 2018. Two weeks later—after serving 22 years in a federal prison—Johnson was granted clemency by the

President and released from prison in June of that year. Johnson was a model prisoner during her time and became an ordained minister while incarcerated.

In order to systematically address the injustices imposed by the 1994 Crime Bill, President Trump signed into law The First Step Act (P.L. 115-391) in December of 2018. The legislation drew widespread, bi-partisan support. This law seeks to improve criminal justice outcomes by creating new mechanisms for maintaining public safety and decreasing the size of the federal prison population.[152] This new law creates incentives for good behavior and participating in rehabilitation programs. Under this new directive, federal inmates convicted of non-violent crimes can earn up to 54 days of credit for every year of their *imposed* sentence, rather than every year of their served sentence.[153] This provision expedites the release of those who demonstrate model behavior, particularly those with extreme sentences.

The First Step Act of 2018 also includes humane measures. For example, the Federal Bureau of Prisons is required to house inmates as close to their primary residence as possible and practical. Some terminally ill and elderly prisoners can be granted home confinement for the remainder of their sentences.[154]

Leo Terrell, a civil rights attorney and lifelong Democrat, commended President Trump and his Administration for doing more for the black community during his first four years in office than all previous administrations combined in the last 50 years.[155]

The Author of Justice

No one cares more for the poor, oppressed, and marginalized than God, the Creator of the universe and Author of mankind. God created social justice—it's called the natural order. God established justice for our protection.

"Learn to do good; seek justice, correct oppression; bring justice to the fatherless, plead the widow's case" (Isaiah 1:17 ESV).

Scripture is clear about the way to achieve justice: do good, avoid evil, and help the oppressed. Justice in the Bible is not a vaguely defined concept; it's a measurement, and The Ten Commandments are the measuring stick. Psalms and Proverbs include many references to "just scales" and "true judgements."

It baffles me how people within our culture—including pastors and spiritual leaders—think that in order to achieve social justice our country needs to fundamentally change. Many church leaders encouraged their congregations to march with Black Lives Matter to protest racial inequality, rather than take solid actions to correct injustice.

There is no greater guide to social justice than the Constitution of the United States, and no other government on the planet that protects human rights more than America. The United States is the only country to offer "equal protection under the law." The idea that you could defend yourself against injustice doesn't even exist in many parts of the world. If you doubt this, I encourage you to speak to those who have fled from Cuba, the Soviet Union, or Iran to come to America.

Could it be that many of our leaders calling for "fundamental change in America" aren't looking for justice, but instead looking for control? Social justice is an intentionally vague concept that can neither be proven nor disproven. It doesn't provide a measuring stick, but instead creates an excuse for violence and vandalism when someone doesn't get their way.

State of the Church

Many churches in America are in a peculiar position right now. By siding with the social justice movement, many have unknowingly engaged in political activism without understanding the implications. At the same time, many of these churches refuse to call out the evils in our society from the pulpit, such as partial-birth abortion and the demonic nature of sex trafficking and pedophilia, for example. Many ministers declined to encourage their congregants to vote—the very foundation of our democratic society—for fear of alienating "the other side." Their silence is deafening.

During the leadup to the presidential election of 2020, Pastor Jeremiah Johnson made a bold declaration:

The Republican National Convention is exposing the cowardice and passivity of the American Church. Is the republican party more awake than the American church? How is the RNC willing to confront issues such as abortion, racism, and bring a clear gospel message, but the church won't? This isn't about being republican or democrat, it's about WHO is willing to boldly address issues from a biblical standard.[156]

To be fair, the modern church movement toward utilizing a corporation-model to establish megachurches and multi-site churches has done a lot to spread the gospel of Jesus Christ and draw in formerly disenfranchised individuals. The American church does a spectacular job of caring for the oppressed. As mentioned in the "Capital Gains" chapter, Christians feed the poor, provide housing for the homeless, and offer services to the underserved all around the world.

But the downside to the expansion of the church in America is the normalization of a Christian subculture that is divorced in many ways from the traditional values the Bible embraces. Christianity used to be inexplicably tied to conservatism; the belief that marriage is between one man and one woman, abortion is murder, there are only two genders, the sexual exploitation of minors (e.g., pedophilia) is to be condemned, and that God is King, not the government. But this is no longer true. Anyone making these claims from the pulpit would be branded as a "hater" or "anti-LGBTQ" and their church would be boycotted or canceled. Pastors are concerned with disenfranchising their members.

Furthermore, the government has set restrictions on our churches, and admittedly, we've allowed it. The 501(c)(3) status sought by churches because of the tax-exempt benefit ties these organizations to more government regulations. This is the exact fear our Founding Fathers addressed in the First Amendment to the Constitution.

Some pastors, however, have spoken out against the government overreach through oppressive lockdowns in the midst of the panic of the global pandemic. Two California pastors—Jack Hibbs of Calvary Chapel in Chino Hills and Rob McCoy of Calvary Chapel in Thousand Oaks—from the Non-Essential Movement (founded by Kirk Cameron and Ryan Higgins) have stood up to protest the infringement of our religious freedoms and to sound a warning against Marxist and socialist ideology creeping into our government.

Other local pastors are taking risks, as well, to stand up for conservative values such as Greg Locke from Global Vision Bible Church and Ron Bailey from New Beginnings Church. Many pastors, however, are choosing to remain silent.

The American church is charging full speed ahead toward the cliff of irrelevance when it refuses to call out blatant immorality in our culture. Local pastors aren't expected to directly impact Hollywood, Wall-Street, or even Washington, DC. They are expected, however, to direct and persuade those sitting in their pews and auditoriums each week. If our religious leaders aren't sounding the alarm to those within their own sphere of influence, our moral compass will forever be tainted.

Policy, more than any other vehicle, profoundly impacts our culture. Consider the enormous influence that the 1962 ruling to end school prayer, the 2014 ruling that the Ten Commandments couldn't be displayed in court buildings, and the 2015 ruling that all same-sex unions must be recognized nationwide had—and still have—on current culture.

The reluctance of the church to engage in the policy discussions further solidifies the Christian subculture. This situation has created several generations of Christians who do not hold—and may not even understand—a biblical worldview. A Barna Group study concluded that only 9% of individuals who identified as born-again Christians identify as having a biblical worldview.[157] *Only 9%.* Your worldview has a profound impact on how you view moral issues and how you perceive truth.

This means that people sitting in church pews and auditoriums week after week are not being instructed on how the Ten Commandments, the teachings of the Prophets, and the Apostle Paul's writings and instructions to new believers should direct how we protect human life, value religious freedom, properly view sexuality, and project these values in our current culture.

Instead, we hear lessons filled with popular psychology on a weekly basis informing us how to become better people and get along with our neighbors. There is nothing wrong with this, of course, but it's only half of the message. God loves justice as much as He does mercy; He promises judgement as much as He promises provision. We're directed to be *both* "innocent as doves" and "shrewd as serpents."[158]

By abdicating our responsibility as Christian leaders to educate those within our circles of influence, the modern American church is culpable of permitting our culture to revert back to the time of the Judges in the Old Testament where "everyone does what is right in his own eyes."[159]

The good news is that revival is coming to America. The bad news is that it may not be coming through the church.

Rogan O'Handley, a former Corporate Finance Attorney and civil rights activist from St. Petersburg, FL said on Instagram, "God is making a comeback in America."[160]

Kayleigh McEnany, the White House Press Secretary under the Trump Administration is very bold about her relationship with Jesus Christ and told CBN news that she believes that God put her in the White House for a reason.[161]

Abby Johnson, former Planned Parenthood Director turned Pro-Life, "I wish people were more concerned about offending the heart of God as they are about offending each other."[162]

Kevin McGary, an Information Technology professional with 35 years of experience in Cybersecurity, Enterprise Applications, and Application Development Automation said this at the Well-Versed Conference in September 2020, "We don't need a racial reconciliation; we need a biblical and spiritual reconciliation."

Bevelyn Beatty, a young black woman in New York City with a troubled past, together with her friend Edmee, poured gallons and gallons of black paint to cover the Black Lives Matter "mural" in downtown Manhattan. Bevelyn and Edmee yelled "only Jesus Matters" while protesting BLM and the Mayor of New York City's disrespect and degradation of their police department.

Even President Trump himself, in one of his campaign rallies in October of 2020, named Jesus Christ and referred to him as "the Boss."

I never thought I would see the day when political activists—not pastors and church leaders—would boldly declare the name of Jesus and the truth of the gospel from the podium. I could never picture how social media (even with all of its ills) and political rallies would be more effective platforms for sharing the Good News than the pulpit. I wouldn't have imagined that a United States President would be a greater champion for the unborn child than the Evangelical Church. President Trump has done more for the Christian community than the Christian church has done for itself.

The Church needs to wake up, or she will be left behind.

The Wrap-Up

The only way to achieve true social justice is to move back *toward* our Constitution—the document founded on the ideals of human rights as presented in Scripture. It is essential that we move *toward* the principles that create law and order, rather than moving further away from it.

Defunding police departments has tragic effects for inner city populations, as history has shown. Many urban communities want more police protection, not less. It would appear that the majority of Americans—particularly the most vulnerable—favor true justice over the vague "philosophical theory" of social justice rooted in revolutionary Communism.

America is headed down a very dark path if we continue to seek "fundamental change" to the rule of law. There is no peace without safety, and there is no safety without justice.

The Lord loves justice. "Turn away from evil and do good; so shall you dwell forever. For the Lord loves justice; he will not forsake his saints. They are preserved forever, but the children of the wicked shall be cut off. The righteous shall inherit the land and dwell upon it forever" (Psalm 37:27–29).

Discussion Guide

Chapter 8: Social Injustice

The purpose of this section is to help you facilitate a meaningful discussion surrounding the material in this chapter.

1. Can you summarize the main idea of this chapter?

2. In your own words, give the definition of social justice.

3. How is social justice the same as or different from justice as defined in Scripture?

4. Do you personally hold a biblical worldview? How does a biblical worldview affect one's attitudes and actions?

5. What does the phrase "equal protection under the law" mean? In which countries does this exist?

6. What are your thoughts about the "defund the police" movement? Would you support it for your city?

Scriptures to read and discuss:

- Isaiah 1:17
- Zechariah 7:9
- Proverbs 28:5
- Proverbs 106:3
- Deuteronomy 16:20
- Psalm 58:11

**Thank you for reading *The Pursuit of Liberty*.
May God richly bless you and may
God bless America.**

Acknowledgments

The concepts in this book developed over many years, long before they were ever written on paper. I would like to thank the following people for making this vision a reality:

- My husband, Perry, for your insights. This couldn't happen without you.

- Tammy Summers, for all the help you provided on this project by advising, and proofreading.

- My advisory committee for your input and guidance: Pastor Mark Lutz, Nick DiRobbio, Nathan Travis, Ruthann Bowen, Valerie Donnelly, Steve Deal, and Connie Geier.

Endnotes

Introduction

1   Margolis, Matt. 2020. "CA Legislature Passes Bill Easing Punishment For Pedophiles Because Of 'LGBTQ Equality' Or Something," Pjmedia.com, https://pjmedia.com/news-and-politics/matt-margolis/2020/09/03/ca-legislature-passes-bill-easing-punishment-for-pedophiles-because-of-lgbtq-equality-or-something-n885940.

Chapter 1

2   "War Of 1812," 2020, American Battlefield Trust, https://www.battlefields.org/learn/war-1812.

3   "Battle Of Fort Mchenry Facts & Summary," 2020, American Battlefield Trust, https://www.battlefields.org/learn/war-1812/battles/fort-mchenry.

4   "Battle Of Fort Mchenry Facts & Summary," 2020, American Battlefield Trust, https://www.battlefields.org/learn/war-1812/battles/fort-mchenry.

5   Allen, Virginia. 2020. "A List Of America's Toppled, Defaced, Or Removed Statues," The Daily Signal, https://www.dailysignal.com/2020/07/17/vandalizing-american-history-a-list-of-64-toppled-defaced-or-removed-statues/.

6   "Sign The Petition," 2019, Change.org,https://www.change.org/p/remove-under-god-from-the-u-s-pledge-of-allegiance.

7   Hicks, Allen. 2020. "What Happened After The Declaration Of Independence Was Signed?", Allanhicks, https://allanhicks.wordpress.com/2012/07/03/what-happened-after-the-declaration-of-independence-was-signed/.

8   Tolles, Frederick. 2020. "William Penn - Founding And Governorship Of Pennsylvania," Encyclopedia Britannica, https://www.britannica.com/biography/William-Penn-English-Quaker-leader-and-colonist/Founding-and-governorship-of-Pennsylvania.

9   "List Of Monuments And Memorials Removed During The George Floyd Protests," 2020, En.Wikipedia.org, https://en.wikipedia.org/wiki/List_of_monuments_and_memorials_removed_during_the_George_Floyd_protests.

10   "SHARIA LAW — LIST OF KEY RULES — What Is
      Sharia Law?", 2019, Billionbibles.org, https://www.billionbi-
      bles.org/sharia/sharia-law.html.

11   @boissolm, Follow, 2020, "The True Story Of The
      Reichstag Fire And The Nazi Rise To Power," Smithsonian
      Magazine, https://www.smithsonianmag.com/history/
      true-story-reichstag-fire-and-nazis-rise-power-180962240/.

12   Ibid

13   Tsarfati, Amir. 2020. Happening Now Jack Hibbs Interview by
      . In person, Calvary Hills Church, Chino Hills, CA.

Chapter 2

14   Publishing, Harvard, 2019, "Marriage And Men's Health -
      Harvard Health," Harvard Health, https://www.health.harvard.
      edu/mens-health/marriage-and-mens-health.

15   Publishing, Harvard, 2019, "Marriage And Men's Health -
      Harvard Health," Harvard Health, https://www.health.harvard.
      edu/mens-health/marriage-and-mens-health.

16   "Love And Money: The Surprising Wealth Predictor |",
      2019, Partners4prosperity.com, https://partners4prosperity.com/
      love-and-money/.

17   Landas, Luke. 2019. "Does Getting Married Increase Wealth
      And Income? - Consumerism Commentary," Consumerism
      Commentary, https://www.consumerismcommentary.com/
      marriage-increase-wealth/.

18   Wandawa, Vicki. 2012. Newvision.Co.Ug, https://www.newvi-
      sion.co.ug/news/1306753/life-orphan-uganda.

19   Parker, Wayne. 2019. "The Troubling Statistics On Fatherless
      Children In America," Liveabout, https://www.liveabout.com/
      fatherless-children-in-america-statistics-1270392.

20   "Statistics," 2018, The Fatherless Generation, https://thefather-
      lessgeneration.wordpress.com/statistics/.

21   "A Christian Catalyst For Change: Jack Brewer's Story,"
      2020, Falkirk Center For Faith & Liberty, https://www.falkirk-
      center.com/2020/04/09/a-christian-catalyst-for-change-jack-
      brewers-story/.

22   "BOP: First Step Act Overview," 2020, Bop.gov, https://www.
      bop.gov/inmates/fsa/overview.jsp.

23 "A Christian Catalyst For Change: Jack Brewer's Story,"
2020, Falkirk Center For Faith & Liberty, https://www.falkirk-center.com/2020/04/09/a-christian-catalyst-for-change-jack-brewers-story/.

24 "The Unauthorized History Of Socialism," 2020, TV
programme, Fox News: Bret Baier,

25 Pletcher, Kenneth. 2020. "One-Child Policy | Definition &
Facts," W88top, http://www.mdc-ds.com/w88top/1794.html.

26 2020, https://blacklivesmatter.com/.

27 Blue Bloods, Season 7, episode 11, 2017.

28 John 8:44

Chapter 3

29 *"Humanae Vitae," The Vatican, July 25, 1968.*

30 "Full Text: Sister Dede Byrne's Speech At The 2020
Republican National Convention," 2020, National Catholic
Register, https://www.ncregister.com/daily-news/full-text-sister-dede-byrnes-speech-at-the-2020-republican-national-convent.

31 "Abolishing Abortion: The History Of The Pro-Life Movement
In America | The American Historian," 2020, Oah.org, https://
www.oah.org/tah/issues/2016/november/abolishing-abortion-the-history-of-the-pro-life-movement-in-america/.

32 "Abortion In The United States By State," 2020, En.
Wikipedia.org, https://en.wikipedia.org/wiki/
Abortion_in_the_United_States_by_state.

33 2020, Plannedparenthood.org.

34 "NPR Choice Page," 2020, Npr.org, https://www.npr.org/
sections/publiceditor/2011/09/19/140612867/abortion-language-politically-correct-or-politically-bomb-throwing#:~:-text=In%20an%20attempt%20to%20be,clinic%22%20are%20
unfair%2C%20too.

35 Rasha, Ali. 2020. Usatoday.com, https://www.usato-day.com/story/life/parenting/2019/09/13/safe-haven-laws-things-you-didnt-know-surrendering-new-born/2031516001/.

36 "The History & Impact Of Planned Parenthood,"
2020, Plannedparenthood.org, https://www.plannedparent-hood.org/about-us/who-we-are/our-history.

37 2020, History.com, https://www.history.com/topics/germany/eugenics.

38 "Negro Project," 2020, Sangervideo.com, http://www.sanger-video.com/negroproject.html.

39 "The Public Papers Of Margaret Sanger: Web Edition," 2020, Nyu.edu, https://www.nyu.edu/projects/sanger/webedition/app/documents/show.php?sangerDoc=306638.xml&_ga=2.28799861.811420770.1598973365-396615015.1598559056.

40 "Negro Project," 2020, Sangervideo.com, http://www.sanger-video.com/negroproject.html.

41 "Negro Project," 2020, Sangervideo.com, http://www.sanger-video.com/negroproject.html.

42 "Kanye West Proclaims Pro-Life Views," 2020, Right To Life UK, https://righttolife.org.uk/news/kanye-west-proclaims-pro-life-views/.

43 "Kanye West Proclaims Pro-Life Views," 2019, Right To Life UK, https://righttolife.org.uk/news/kanye-west-proclaims-pro-life-views/.

44 "Klassen: Kanye West Is Changing The Face Of The Pro-Life Movement - Alpha News," 2020, Alpha News, https://alphanewsmn.com/klassen-kanye-west-is-changing-the-face-of-the-pro-life-movement/.

45 "Kanye West Proclaims Pro-Life Views," 2019, Right To Life UK, https://righttolife.org.uk/news/kanye-west-proclaims-pro-life-views/.

46 Harris, David J. 2018. Why I Couldn't Stay Silent, DJHJ Media, LLC.

47 Harris, David J. 2018. Why I Couldn't Stay Silent, DJHJ Media, LLC.

48 Ingles, Jo. 2019. "In 2019, Ohio Passed Its Most Restrictive Abortion Law In Modern History," Radio,Wosu.org, https://radio.wosu.org/post/2019-ohio-passed-its-most-restrictive-abortion-law-modern-history#stream/0.

Chapter 4

49 Sopelsa, Brooke. 2020. "Amy Coney Barrett Apologizes For Use Of Phrase 'Sexual Preference,'" NBC News, https://www.nbcnews.com/feature/nbc-out/amy-coney-barrett-apologizes-use-phrase-sexual-preference-n1243285.

50   Ibid

51   Murphee, Randall. 2020. "AFA Journal - Pediatrician
      Champions Truth Versus Transgender Insanity," AFA
      Journal, https://afajournal.org/past-issues/2020/may/
      pediatrician-champions-truth-versus-transgender-insanity/.

52   "What Is Gender Dysphoria?", 2019, Psychiatry.org, https://
      www.psychiatry.org/patients-families/gender-dysphoria/
      what-is-gender-dysphoria.

53   Dolphins, Jotaro. 2020. "Complete List Of Genders - The
      Complete List Of All Genders – Wattpad," Wattpad.com,
      https://www.wattpad.com/341462536-complete-list-of-gen-
      ders-the-complete-list-of-all.

54   Ibid

55   Desanctis, Alexandra. 2020. "'Sex'- Trump Administration
      Reverses Obama-Era Regulation That Redefined Term
      | National Review," Nationalreview.com, https://www.
      nationalreview.com/2020/06/trump-administration-revers-
      es-obama-era-regulation-that-redefined-sex/.

56   Vitale, Ali. 2017. "White House Rolls Back Obama-Era
      Transgender Bathroom Protections," NBC News, https://
      www.nbcnews.com/politics/white-house/white-house-revers-
      es-obama-era-transgender-bathroom-protections-n724426.

57   Vitale, Ali. 2017. "White House Rolls Back Obama-Era
      Transgender Bathroom Protections," NBC News, https://
      www.nbcnews.com/politics/white-house/white-house-revers-
      es-obama-era-transgender-bathroom-protections-n724426.

58   Desanctis, Alexandra. 2020. "'Sex'- Trump Administration
      Reverses Obama-Era Regulation That Redefined Term
      | National Review," Nationalreview.com, https://www.
      nationalreview.com/2020/06/trump-administration-revers-
      es-obama-era-regulation-that-redefined-sex/.

59   Ellis Nutt, Amy. 2017. https://omaha.com/livewellnebraska/
      health/johns-hopkins-will-resume-gender-reassignment-sur-
      geries-after--year/article_0c370372-1aee-11e7-8049-d3ae-
      3854aff5.html?utm_medium=social&utm_source=email&utm_
      campaign=user-share.

60   Ellis Nutt, Amy. 2017. https://omaha.com/livewellnebraska/
      health/johns-hopkins-will-resume-gender-reassignment-sur-
      geries-after--year/article_0c370372-1aee-11e7-8049-d3ae-
      3854aff5.html?utm_medium=social&utm_source=email&utm_
      campaign=user-share.

61   Heyer, Walt. 2018. "9 Trans Patients Lodge Shocking Complaints About Sex-Change Surgeries," The Federalist, https://thefederalist.com/2018/12/06/9-transgender-patients-complain-mutilation-botched-sex-change-surgeries-oregon/.

62   Segar, Mike. 2020. "Joe Biden Says Young Children Who Decide They 'Want To Be Transgender' Should Face 'Zero Discrimination,'" RT International, https://www.rt.com/usa/503659-biden-child-transgenderism-claims/.

63   Ibid

64   Eaton-Robb, Pat. 2019. "Transgender Sprinters Finish 1St, 2Nd At Connecticut Girls Indoor Track Championships," The Washington Times, https://www.washingtontimes.com/news/2019/feb/24/terry-miller-andraya-yearwood-transgender-sprinter/.

65   Carlson, Tucker. 2018. "Twitter," Twitter.com, https://twitter.com/tuckercarlson/status/948370452656861186?lang=en.

Chapter 5

66   "More Poverty Than Ever Before |", 2020, Therealcuba.com, https://therealcuba.com/?page_id=273.

67   Fox Nation, Bair, Brett, 2020, The Unauthorized History Of Socialism, Video, https://nation.foxnews.com/watch/fe54b3f144aa809b875c147c037c2fa9/.

68   Smithha, Frank. 2018. "Socialist Experiment In Tanzania: 1961-85," Fsmitha.com, http://www.fsmitha.com/h2/ch34-tan.htm.

69   Fox Nation, Bair, Brett, 2020, The Unauthorized History Of Socialism, Video.

70   "Top 5 Failed Socialist Promises: From Lenin To Chavez," 2020, Fox News, https://www.foxnews.com/politics/top-5-failed-socialist-promises-from-lenin-to-chavez.

71   Cohen, Luc. 2020. "Explainer: Why Oil-Rich Venezuela Is Suffering Severe Gasoline Shortages," U.S., https://www.reuters.com/article/us-venezuela-gasoline-explainer-idUSKBN22V32G.

72   Sequera, Vivian. 2018. "Venezuelans Report Big Weight Losses In 2017 As Hunger Hits," U.S., https://www.reuters.com/article/us-venezuela-food-idUSKCN1G52HA.

73 Margolis, Jason. 2019. "Venezuela Was Once The Richest, Most Stable, Democracy In Latin America. What Happened?", The World From PRX, https://www.pri.org/stories/2019-02-07/venezuela-was-once-richest-most-stable-democracy-latin-america-what-happened.

74 https://www.businessinsider.com/alexandria-ocasio-cortez-explains-what-democratic-socialism-means-2019-3?op=1

75 Administration, Veterans, 2020, "VA.gov | Veterans Affairs," Va.vov, https://www.va.gov/health/.

76 "'SEAL Team' Exposes VA: 'A Health Care System That Runs Like The Post Office,'" 2019, Newsbusters, https://www.newsbusters.org/blogs/culture/lindsay-kornick/2019/04/25/seal-team-exposes-va-health-care-system-runs-post-office.

77 "Barack Obama VA Scandal: 6 Facts About Veterans Health Administration Controversy," Newsmax, Newsmax Media, Inc., 22 Dec. 2014, www.newsmax.com/FastFeatures/barack-obama-scandal-facts/2014/12/22/id/613907/.

78 "Economy Of Sweden," 2020, En.Wikipedia.org, https://en.wikipedia.org/wiki/Economy_of_Sweden.

79 Feld, Stanley, 2020, "Swedes Are Frustrated Over Their Socialized Healthcare System," Repairing The Healthcare System, https://stanleyfeldmdmace.typepad.com/repairing_the_healthcare_/2020/01/swedes-are-frustrated-over-their-socialized-healthcare-system-.html.

80 Hjertqvist, Johan. 2015. Thelocal.Se, https://www.thelocal.se/20150127/swedens-health-care-is-a-shame-to-the-country.

81 Hjertqvist, Johan. 2015. Thelocal.Se, https://www.thelocal.se/20150127/swedens-health-care-is-a-shame-to-the-country.

82 Pour, Nima. 2020. "Sweden And Its Welfare State In Crisis," Gatestone Institute, https://www.gatestoneinstitute.org/15414/sweden-welfare-crisis.

83 Ibid

84 Hjertqvist, Johan. 2015. Thelocal.Se, https://www.thelocal.se/20150127/swedens-health-care-is-a-shame-to-the-country.

85 "Boris Johnson | Biography, Facts, & Role In Brexit," 2020, Encyclopedia Britannica. https://www.britannica.com/biography/Boris-Johnson.

86 2020, History.com, https://www.history.com/topics/british-history/margaret-thatcher.

87   2 Thessalonians 3:10

88   Kirk, C. 2020. October 11, "Was Jesus a Solialist," [Instagram Post], Phoenix, AZ: Turning Point USA.

89   "Why Socialism Always Results In Tyrannical Rule," 1998, Orthodoxnet.com, https://www.orthodoxnet.com/news/WhySocialismAlwaysResultsInTyranny.html.

90   "Friedrich Hayek," 2020, En.Wikipedia.org, https://en.wikipedia.org/wiki/Friedrich_Hayek.

Chapter 6

91   "Uzbekistan," 2020, En.Wikipedia.org, https://en.wikipedia.org/wiki/Uzbekistan.

92   Griffin, Chris. 2020. Uzbekistan and their Quest for Religious Freedom, Interview by Amy L. Travis, Interview, In person, PIttsburgh, PA.

93   Ibid

94   Fox Nation, Bair, Brett, 2020, The Unauthorized History Of Socialism, Video.

95   Silver, Caleb. 2020. "The Top 20 Economies In The World," Investopedia, https://www.investopedia.com/insights/worlds-top-economies/#1-united-states.

96   Gye, Hugo. 2020. "America IS The 1%: You Need Just $34,000 Annual Income To Be In The Global Elite... And HALF The World's Richest People Live In The U.S.," Mail Online, https://www.dailymail.co.uk/news/article-2082385/We-1--You-need-34k-income-global-elite--half-worlds-richest-live-U-S.html.

97   Albrecht, Leslie. 2020. "The U.S. Is The No. 1 Most Generous Country In The World For The Last Decade," Marketwatch, https://www.marketwatch.com/story/the-us-is-the-most-generous-country-but-americans-say-debt-is-keeping-them-from-giving-more-to-charity-2019-10-18.

98   Albrecht, Leslie. 2020. "The U.S. Is The No. 1 Most Generous Country In The World For The Last Decade," Marketwatch, https://www.marketwatch.com/story/the-us-is-the-most-generous-country-but-americans-say-debt-is-keeping-them-from-giving-more-to-charity-2019-10-18.

99   Rezaian, Jason. 2020. https://www.washingtonpost.com/opinions/2020/05/28/how-immigrant-ingenuity-is-helping-restaurants-rise-pandemic-challenge/.

100   2020, Optimistdaily.com, https://www.optimistdaily.
      com/2020/04/the-clever-strategies-small-businesses-are-us-
      ing-to-survive-quarantine/.

101   "Bottled Water History," 2020, Nestlé Waters US., https://
      www.nestle-watersna.com/who-we-are/our-history/
      bottledwaterhistory.

102   Mentioff, Rachel. 2019. "Maryland Students' Reading
      Proficiency Scores Drop In 2019," Baltimore.Cbslocal.
      com, https://baltimore.cbslocal.com/2019/10/30/
      baltimore-maryland-education-nations-report-card/.

103   Ibid

104   Papst, Chris. 2020. "13 Baltimore City High Schools, Zero
      Students Proficient In Math," WBFF, https://foxbaltimore.
      com/news/project-baltimore/13-baltimore-city-high-schools-
      zero-students-proficient-in-math.

105   Durden, Tyler. 2020. "End School To Prison Pipeline'
      - New Kim Klacik Ad Highlights How Liberals Destroyed
      Baltimore," Zero Hedge, https://www.zerohedge.com/political/
      end-school-prison-pipeline-new-kim-klacik-ad-highlights-
      how-liberals-destroyed-baltimore.

106   "Bernie Madoff | Biography, Ponzi Scheme, & Facts,"
      2020, Encyclopedia Britannica, https://www.britannica.com/
      biography/Bernie-Madoff.

107   Kenton, Will. 2020. "Trickle-Down Theory," Investopedia,
      https://www.investopedia.com/terms/t/trickledowntheory.asp.

108   Talgo, Chris. 2019. "From JFK To Trump: 'A Rising Tide (Of
      Free-Market Policies) Lifts All Boats,'" Townhall, https://
      townhall.com/columnists/christalgo/2019/07/24/jfk-to-trump-
      a-rising-tide-of-freemarket-policies-lifts-all-boats-n2550472.

109   "JFK - 'A Rising Tide Raises All The Boats" - Phrase Meaning
      And Origin," 2020, Phrases.org.Uk, https://www.phrases.org.
      uk/bulletin_board/42/messages/1052.html.

110   "In Portland, Protests And Violence Continue -- 3 Months
      After They Began," 2020, PBS Newshour, https://www.pbs.org/
      newshour/show/in-portland-protests-and-violence-continue-3-
      months-after-they-began.

111   2020, Usatoday.com, https://www.usatoday.com/story/
      opinion/2020/07/03/police-black-killings-homicide-rates-race-
      injustice-column/3235072001/.

112   Volanti, Dr. John. 2020. "PTSD Among Police Officers: Impact On Critical Decision Making," Cops.Usdoj.gov, https://cops.usdoj.gov/html/dispatch/05-2018/PTSD.html.

113   2020, Forbes.com, https://www.forbes.com/athletes/#193b5f3d55ae.

Chapter 7

114   Chapman, Michael. 2020. "FLASHBACK: Morgan Freeman On Ending Racism: 'Stop Talking About It' -- Black History Month Is 'Ridiculous,'" Cnsnews.com, https://www.cnsnews.com/blog/michael-w-chapman/flashback-morgan-freeman-ending-racism-stop-talking-about-it-black-history.

115   Maher, Gary. 2020. "Morgan Freeman Drops Truth Bomb On Race Hustlers Leaving CNN Embarrassed & Speechless!", USA Politics Today, https://www.usapoliticstoday.org/morgan-freeman-drops-truth-bomb/.

116   "<P>10 Black Celebrities Who Have Said Questionable Things About Racism</P>", 2016, Essence, https://www.essence.com/celebrity/black-celebrities-racism-doesnt-exist/#82500.

117   2019, History.com, https://www.history.com/topics/early-20th-century-us/jim-crow-laws.

118   Urofsky, Melvin. 2020. "Jim Crow Law | History, Facts, & Examples," Encyclopedia Britannica, https://www.britannica.com/event/Jim-Crow-law.

119   2009, History.com, https://www.history.com/topics/black-history/plessy-v-ferguson.

120   2020, History.com, https://www.history.com/topics/black-history/brown-v-board-of-education-of-topeka.

121   "Browder V. Gayle Filed - African American Registry," 2020, African American Registry, https://aaregistry.org/story/browder-v-gayle-filed/.

122   "Oprah Winfrey," 2020, Biography, https://www.biography.com/media-figure/oprah-winfrey.

123   "7 Richest Most Powerful Ethnic Groups In America," 2018, Insider Monkey, https://www.insidermonkey.com/blog/7-richest-most-powerful-ethnic-groups-in-america-653720/7/.

124   "Economic Opportunity Act Of 1964," 2020, En.Wikipedia.org, https://en.wikipedia.org/wiki/Economic_Opportunity_Act_of_1964.

125 "Black America Before LBJ's &Quot;Great Society&Quot;: How The Welfare State Helped Ruin Black Communities," 2020, Ammo.com, https://ammo.com/articles/lbj-great-society-war-on-poverty-welfare-state-helped-ruin-black-communities.

126 Delmont, Matthew. 2020. "What Black Americans Lost By Aligning With The Democrats," The Atlantic, https://www.theatlantic.com/politics/archive/2016/03/exit-left/476190/.

127 Ibid

128 "Reagan Condemns Welfare System, Says It's Made Poverty Worse Instead Of Better," 2020, Los Angeles Times, https://www.latimes.com/archives/la-xpm-1986-02-16-mn-8585-story.html.

129 "African-American Family Structure," 2018, En.Wikipedia.org, https://en.wikipedia.org/wiki/African-American_family_structure.

130 "3 Ways The 1994 Crime Bill Continues To Hurt Communities Of Color - Center For American Progress," 2018, Center For American Progress, https://www.american-progress.org/issues/race/news/2019/05/10/469642/3-ways-1994-crime-bill-continues-hurt-communities-color/.

131 School, Stanford, 2020, "Three Strikes Basics | Stanford Law School," Stanford Law School, https://law.stanford.edu/stanford-justice-advocacy-project/three-strikes-basics/.

132 Instagram post from Joelpatrick1776, August 28, 2020.

133 Instagram post from Joelpatrick1776, October 15, 2020.

134 Instagram post from Dineshjdsouza, August 9, 2020.

135 "America The Least Racist Country - Www.Elizabethton.com," 2020, https://www.elizabethton.com/2020/06/09/america-the-least-racist-country/.

Chapter 8

136 Cunningham, William. 2020. "Black Lives Matter: Corporate America Has Pledged $1.678 Billion So Far," Black Enterprise, https://www.blackenterprise.com/black-lives-matter-corporate-america-has-pledged-1-678-billion-so-far/.

137 Pavlich, Katie. 2020. "Cost Of Recent Riot Damages Are The Worst In U.S. History," Townhall, https://townhall.com/tipsheet/katiepavlich/2020/09/16/the-financial-cost-of-recent-riots-has-been-tabulated-n2576294.

138   Ibid

139   "Social Justice Definition," 2020, Investopedia. https://www.investopedia.com/terms/s/social-justice.asp.

140   2020, https://www.wtsp.com/article/features/defund-the-police-origin/67-9271557c-89e0-48ab-8e45-fa0dd1ae9c09.

141   Ibid

142   Ibid

143   GRZESZCZAK, JOCELYN. 2020. "81% Of Black Americans Don't Want Less Police Presence Despite Protests—Some Want More Cops: Poll," Newsweek, https://www.newsweek.com/81-black-americans-dont-want-less-police-presence-despite-protestssome-want-more-cops-poll-1523093.

144   "Memphis, TN Crime Rates And Statistics – Neighborhood scout," 2020, Neighborhoodscout.com, https://www.neighborhoodscout.com/tn/memphis/crime#data.

145   McCarthy, Niall. 2020. "Major American Cities See Sharp Spike In Murders In 2020 [Infographic]," Forbes, https://www.forbes.com/sites/niallmccarthy/2020/08/04/major-american-cities-see-sharp-spike-in-murders-in-2020-infographic/?sh=33f94b5b5af2.

146   Hart, Kim. 2020. "The Cities That Are Already Defunding The Police," Axios, https://www.axios.com/cities-defund-the-police-george-floyd-188e169a-a32a-44fa-bace-e2e5df4d1c9b.html.

147   McCarthy, Niall. 2020. "Major American Cities See Sharp Spike In Murders In 2020 [Infographic]," Forbes, https://www.forbes.com/sites/niallmccarthy/2020/08/04/major-american-cities-see-sharp-spike-in-murders-in-2020-infographic/?sh=33f94b5b5af2.

148   Hart, Kim. 2020. "The Cities That Are Already Defunding The Police," Axios, https://www.axios.com/cities-defund-the-police-george-floyd-188e169a-a32a-44fa-bace-e2e5df4d1c9b.html.

149   Graves, Lucia. 2011. "Huffpost Is Now A Part Of Verizon Media," Huffpost.com, https://www.huffpost.com/entry/crack-powder-sentencing-d_n_667317.

150   Ibid

151   "Alice Marie Johnson," 2020, En.Wikipedia.org, https://en.wikipedia.org/wiki/Alice_Marie_Johnson.

152   "BOP: First Step Act Overview," 2020, Bop.gov, https://www.bop.gov/inmates/fsa/overview.jsp.

153 Ibid

154 Ibid

155 Elliot, Chris. 2020. "Civil Rights Attorney, Lifelong Democrat: President Trump Has Done More For Blacks Than Obama," Law Enforcement Today, https://www.lawenforcementtoday.com/civil-rights-attorney-trump-has-done-more-for-blacks-than-obama/.

156 Johnson, Jeremiah. 2020. "Jeremiah Johnson Ministries On Facebook Watch," Facebook Watch, https://www.facebook.com/watch/live/?v=638558523748627&ref=watch_permalink.

157 "A Biblical Worldview Has A Radical Effect On A Person's Life - Barna Group," 2003, Barna Group.

158 Matthew 10:16

159 Judges 17:6

160 September 19, 2020

161 Brody, David. 2020. "'I Believe God Put Me In This Place For A Purpose': New WH Press Secretary On Faith, Love Of Country, And Overcoming Adversity," CBN News, https://www1.cbn.com/cbnnews/us/2020/may/i-believe-god-put-me-in-this-place-for-a-purpose-new-wh-press-secretary-on-faith-love-of-country-and-overcoming-adversity.

162 Instagram @AbbyJohnson on 11/12/20.Contact the Author

Contact the Author

For questions or to order multiple books, please contact Amy at atravisconsulting@gmail.com. Discounts are available for bulk orders.

Visit her website at www.amytravisunlimited.com.

Amy L. Travis
Owner, Fusion Publishing